THE AUTOGRAPH BOOK OF L.A.

Actress Rita Hayworth autographs a golden shoe, 1945.

THE AUTOGRAPH BOOK OF L.A.

IMPROVEMENTS ON THE PAGE OF THE CITY

JOSH KUN

FOREWORD BY JOHN F. SZABO

INTRODUCTION BY SHEPARD FAIREY

CAPTIONS BY FRANCES CORRY

INSPIRED BY THE AUTOGRAPH COLLECTION
OF THE LOS ANGELES PUBLIC LIBRARY

ACP
ANGEL CITY PRESS

LOS ANGELES
PUBLIC LIBRARY

Library
Foundation
of Los Angeles

Los Angeles Public Library

Autographs

I would just like to be part of it.

David Gurnick
Chatsworth
June 2, 2018

DAVID GURNICK, 2018

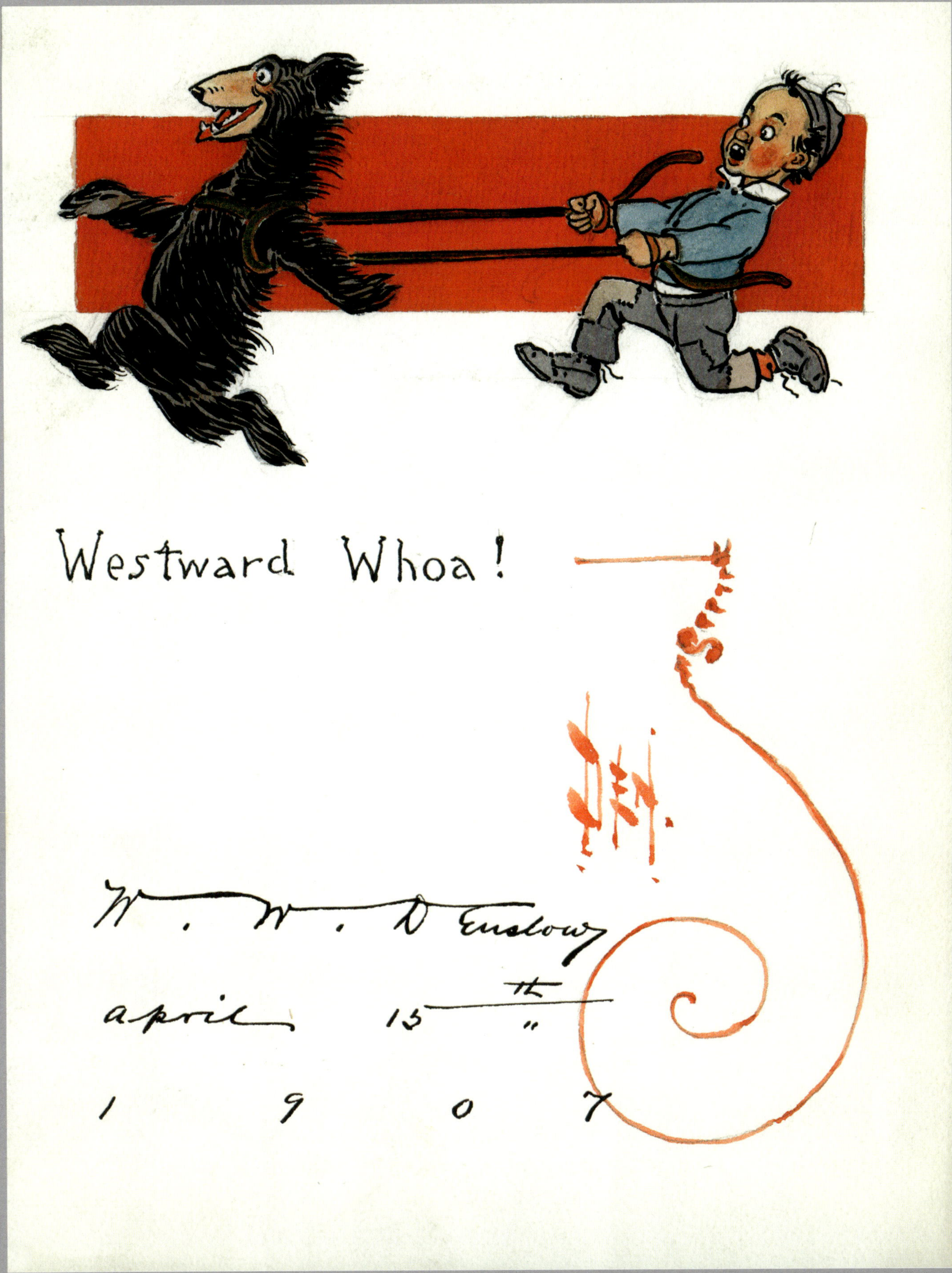

W.W. DENSLOW, 1907

An animal hide filled with signatures in the Tom Mix Western Museum of the San Fernando Valley, 1947.

POR FAVOR
MILTON UHLER
JACK MOSS
BUCK JONES
ELDON MILLER

Signing a fellow student's "doodle skirt" at Birmingham High School in Van Nuys, 1955.

CONTENTS

AUTHOR'S NOTE JOSH KUN 10

FOREWORD JOHN F. SZABO 14

INTRODUCTION SHEPARD FAIREY 24

THE AUTOGRAPH BOOK OF L.A. 32

DISPATCHES FROM THE CITY BENEATH SUSAN A. PHILLIPS 82

RIVER BED ROLL CALLS CHAZ BOJÓRQUEZ 98

IMPROVEMENTS ON THE PAGE OF THE CITY: A GALLERY 106

ENDNOTES 218
ACKNOWLEDGMENTS 220
AUTOGRAPH INDEX 221
CREDITS 223

AUTHOR'S NOTE

THE AUTOGRAPH BOOK OF L.A. is the third and final volume in my series of books inspired by the special collections of Los Angeles Public Library, and yet it feels more like an introduction than a conclusion.

Where *Songs in the Key of Los Angeles* and *To Live and Dine in L.A.* were rooted in single collections of sheet music and restaurant menus, respectively, *The Autograph Book of L.A.* is more omnivorous. It begins with the Charles Lummis Autograph Collection begun in 1906 but then fans outward to include related materials from other LAPL collections throughout the last century. It is driven less by the stories contained in a solitary archive of objects and more by a guiding argument, one that runs through all three projects in different ways. The argument goes something like this: the cultural archives of Los Angeles are powerful windows into the uneven cultural politics of the past (Whose stories are preserved? Whose are forgotten or erased?), but also into the uneven cultural politics of the present (Whose experiences circulate, flourish, and are made visible? Whose are displaced, ignored, and dislodged?). While *Songs* and *To Live and Dine* reveled in the glories and pleasures of the L.A. past—a song about an orange grove, a menu from the Brown Derby—they used that documented past to pose larger questions about what archives reveal and what they obscure, and what those inclusions and absences tell us about the present and future of the city. When I showed Chef Roy Choi some of the Library's most treasured and historic nineteenth-century menus—elegant New Year's Eve dinners, lavish hotel banquets—he replied, "These are great, but where did everybody else eat?"

In each project, the aim has been not to merely reproduce these magnificent artifacts and ephemera that hold so much of our city's history, but to use them as tools for critical thinking about that history. Working closely with librarians, as well as with musicians, chefs, organizers, and artists across the city, my goal also has been to animate the Library's special collections by bringing them to life in new contemporary contexts, with the explicit aim of *de-specializing* them, of returning their stories to the living, collective imagination of the city's many communities. What happens when contemporary musicians interpret songs from the 1920s about eternal sunshine or Old Mexico? What do we learn about food inequality and food insecurity when contemporary chefs respond to vintage menus? And now, what do turn-of-the-twentieth-century autographs tell us about the power of names and naming? About what it means for anyone to leave their mark on the city they call *home*?

Musicians have signature pieces and phrasing. Chefs have signature dishes. In *The Autograph Book of L.A.*, the signature itself, and all of its meanings and resonances, is at the center: who is asked to leave it, where can it be left, and which signatures are allowed to outlast the hands that draw them? Just as sheet music and restaurant menus helped reflect histories of power, urban inequity, racism, migration and deportation, urban development, gentrification, and displacement, so too do autographs—historical and contemporary alike. They turn our attention to social, cultural, political, and economic issues that go far beyond the traces left by fountain pens, felt-tip markers, and aerosol cans.

To conclude the sheet-music project, we threw a massive free public concert that asked nearly five thousand Angelenos to sing along with the past while creating new harmonies for the present. In the exhibition that accompanied *To Live and Dine in L.A.*, we provided blank restaurant menus and asked gallery visitors to write their own food histories of Los Angeles. To launch this project, we held an Autograph Day at branch libraries and invited everyone in the city to add their autographs to the Library's collection.

I see all three of these books—and their accompanying recordings, exhibitions, and public programs—as united in the pursuit of a critically minded public history. As Dolores Hayden famously asked many years ago when she researched the layers of obscured history and struggle that went into the making of Little Tokyo, the Embassy Auditorium, and Biddy Mason's homestead, what does a socially inclusive urban history look like? My hope is that *The Autograph Book of L.A.* joins preceding volumes in helping to answer that question.

At the back of this book there are blank autograph pages. They are meant to serve as a reminder that the history of Los Angeles remains unwritten and will forever be co-authored by its residents, that the pages of the city continue to turn. They are ready to be marked up. They are hungry for names the city does not yet know. They await all of our autographs, yours especially.

—J.K.

Graffiti adorns the embankments of the Los Angeles River near Burbank, 1991.

Dodgers third baseman Ron Cey signs a fan's autograph book, 1981.

FOREWORD

JOHN F. SZABO, CITY LIBRARIAN

RICHARD ELWOOD DODGE, 1907

Grip, the 175-year-old stuffed raven and former pet of Charles Dickens.

The Reverend Dr. Martin Luther King Jr.'s childhood library card.

A scarf worn by Amelia Earhart in her early days as a pilot in North Hollywood.

EACH OF THESE TREASURES CAN BE FOUND in the collections of public libraries in Philadelphia, Atlanta, and Los Angeles, respectively. They exemplify the diverse and often eclectic nature of special collections within the people's university.

The highly specialized collections of public libraries—like the DC Punk Archive at District of Columbia Public Library, the Léda Hincks Plauché Collection of Mardi Gras Costume and Float Designs at New Orleans Public Library, the Shades of L.A. Photography Collection at Los Angeles Public Library, and the Claude F. Bloodgood Chess Collection at Cleveland Public Library—help preserve community history and tell vital stories. This is a core and critically important mission of libraries.

Collections form in many ways; some special collections are donated in whole or in part, and they often arrive through unexpected paths. Other collections sometimes begin as the particular interest of an individual librarian, as is the case with Los Angeles Public Library's notable and endlessly charming Autograph Collection. Begun more than 110 years ago, the collection helps us better understand the early twentieth century and what was important to Los Angeles; the Library; and its tenth city librarian, Charles Fletcher Lummis, who initiated the collection. An eccentric raconteur and early scrapbooker of sorts, Lummis sought to elevate Los Angeles Public Library's national prominence, and likely his own, by convincing "people who count" to "improve upon a page" of fresh library stationery.

From poet Katherine Lee Bates's handwritten lyrics of "America the Beautiful" to cartoonist Grant Hamilton's whimsical tube of paint spilling onto the page like an early tease of pop art, the responses to Lummis's call were often playful, surprising, and undoubtedly reflective of the contributor's personality and the impression they wished to make.

Over the last century, there have been sporadic but noteworthy additions to the Autograph Collection, perhaps most memorable being the poem "Youth" written by Langston Hughes in his own hand in 1935. The collection also includes a poem by Hughes's friend and fellow member of the Harlem Renaissance Arna Wendell Bontemps, as well as correspondence from author and activist Helen Keller.

ABBY SANCHEZ, 2018

When this project began, we knew we wanted to democratize and diversify the collection to better reflect the role of libraries in the twenty-first century and the many communities we serve today. In the summer of 2018, we hosted Autograph Day at nineteen of our neighborhood libraries, inviting every patron who walked in to take a sheet of the blank Library stationery we'd reproduced and submit a signature, a message, or a work of art that would become part of our special collection. What rich treasures we collected, as Angelenos responded with heartfelt expressions of themselves.

More than anything, public libraries are about the people who use them. Special collections are a way we preserve the stories of the communities where our patrons live and ensure that those stories are told and retold. This is true of the autographs in this book and the "improvements to the page" Lummis requested, as well as those contributions by the hundreds of Angelenos who participated in our most recent solicitation and left a mark uniquely their own.

That these extraordinary special collections are birthed, sustained, and preserved across generations is a testament to the dedication and perseverance of librarians and archivists, as well as to the permanence of our institutions and the values they represent. The caretakers of these special collections in America's public libraries are as committed to serving the sixth grader working on a history-fair project as they are to the scholar doing research. Accessibility and discoverability are of primary importance, and librarians work to have these collections searchable and readily accessible through national and global discovery platforms.

The accessibility and discoverability of the Autograph Collection has now been greatly enhanced by *The Autograph Book of L.A.* The book's breadth of vision comes from the brilliant and multitalented Josh Kun, who, in partnership with Angel City Press, has now completed a trilogy of splendid, beautiful works that explore the most enchanting collections of Los Angeles Public Library. His work was informed by the deeply committed librarians Kren Malone, Ani Boyadjian, Madeline Bryant, and Xochitl Oliva, who provided both access and insight into the collections. These pages also reflect the curiosity and intellect of Todd Lerew of the Library Foundation of Los Angeles, who has shaped both the book and the larger, Library-wide project that surrounds it.

Most significantly, this book has been transformed by each of the diverse patrons of the Library, who—through their participation and use of our collections, services, programs, spaces, and resources—leave their own mark and help to ensure that our libraries can continue to safeguard and celebrate stories large and small for generations to come.

John F. Szabo
City Librarian
Los Angeles Public Library

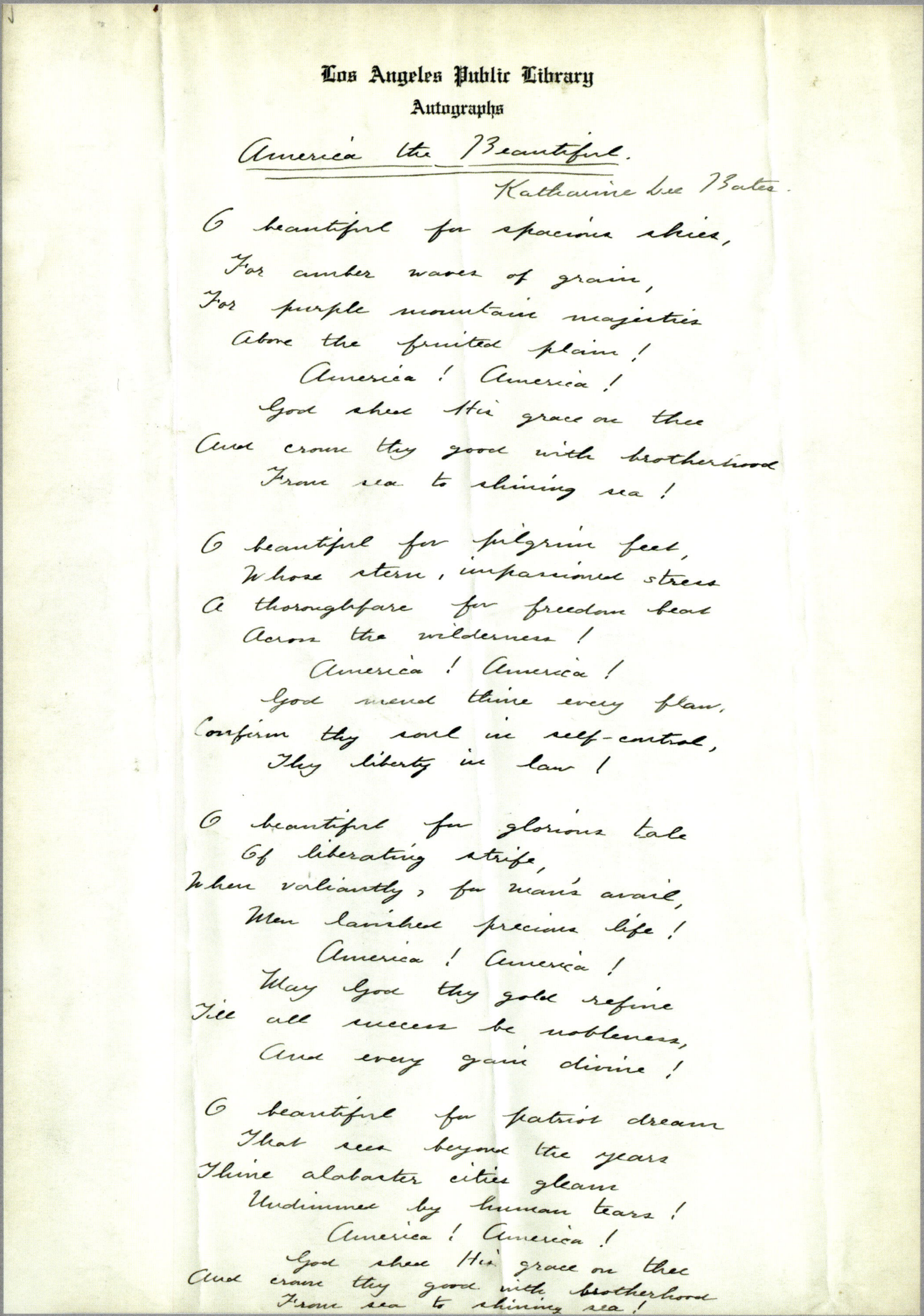

Los Angeles Public Library

Autographs

America the Beautiful.

Katharine Lee Bates.

O beautiful for spacious skies,
For amber waves of grain,
For purple mountain majesties
Above the fruited plain!
America! America!
God shed His grace on thee
And crown thy good with brotherhood
From sea to shining sea!

O beautiful for pilgrim feet,
Whose stern, impassioned stress
A thoroughfare for freedom beat
Across the wilderness!
America! America!
God mend thine every flaw,
Confirm thy soul in self-control,
Thy liberty in law!

O beautiful for glorious tale
Of liberating strife,
When valiantly, for man's avail,
Men lavished precious life!
America! America!
May God thy gold refine
Till all success be nobleness,
And every gain divine!

O beautiful for patriot dream
That sees beyond the years
Thine alabaster cities gleam
Undimmed by human tears!
America! America!
God shed His grace on thee
And crown thy good with brotherhood
From sea to shining sea!

KATHARINE LEE BATES, early 1900s • "America the Beautiful" lyrics

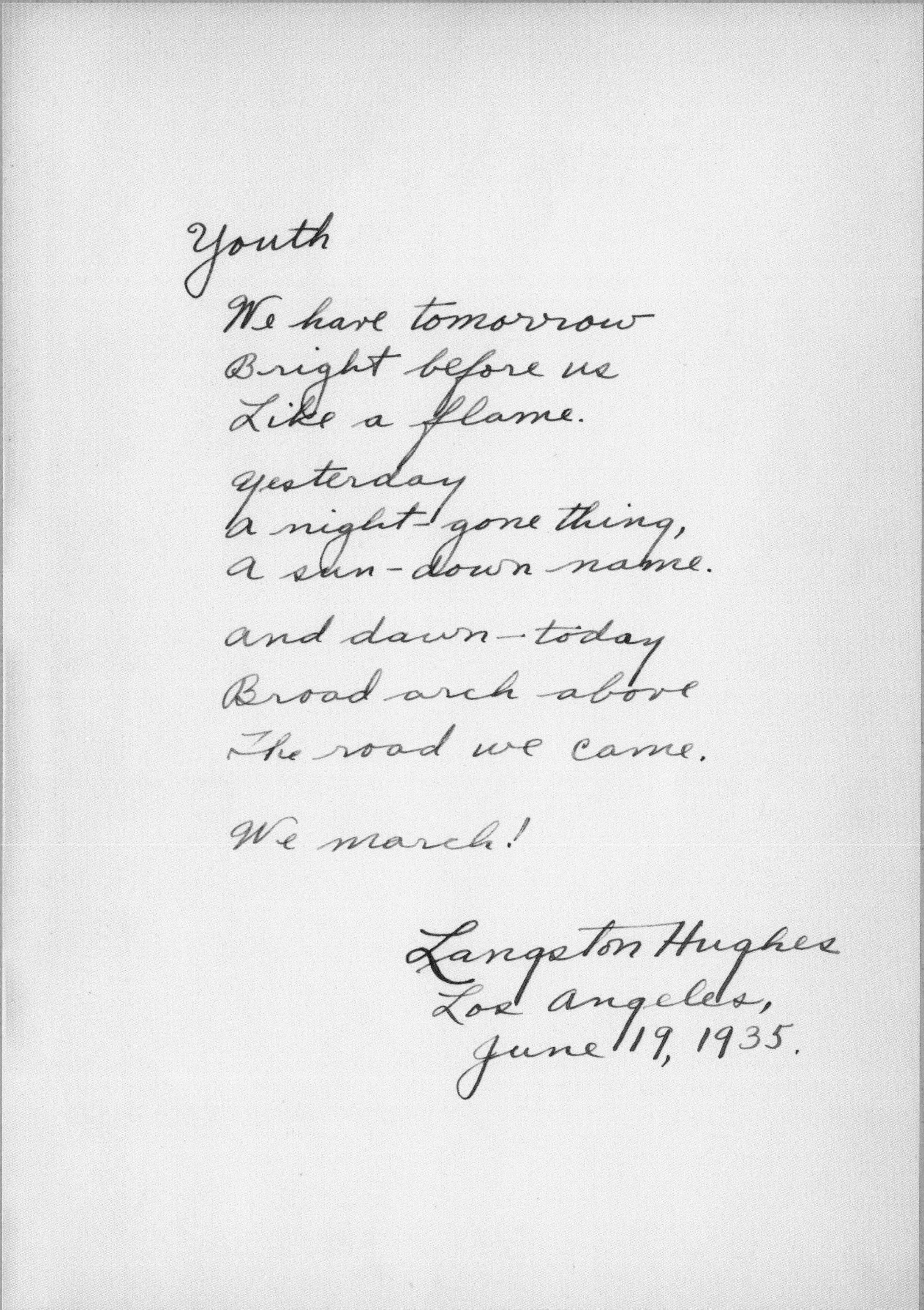

Youth

We have tomorrow
Bright before us
Like a flame.

Yesterday
a night-gone thing,
a sun-down name.

and dawn-today
Broad arch above
The road we came.

We march!

Langston Hughes
Los Angeles,
June 19, 1935.

LANGSTON HUGHES, 1935 • "Youth" We have tomorrow / Bright before us / Like a flame. / Yesterday / a night-gone thing, / a sun-down name. / and dawn-today / Broad arch above / The road we came. / We march!

AUTOGRAPHS o

These are so
hand and foot
court of the C

A souvenir autograph book from Grauman's Chinese Theatre in Hollywood lists those who have left their mark in its concrete blocks, including Shirley Temple, Clark Gable, and Fred Astaire, 1938.

Hedy Lamarr signs an autograph book at the El Capitan Theatre in Hollywood, 1940.

INTRODUCTION

SHEPARD FAIREY

A Forest Service ranger sandblasts graffiti from a rock near the San Gabriel River, 1989.

THE IDEA OF THE AUTOGRAPH IS MULTI-LAYERED. When you ask someone who is famous for their autograph, their signature—whether it's beautiful, stylish, or calligraphic—becomes a symbol of everything that person has accomplished. Getting an autograph from someone is special because you will know forever that the writing came directly from that person's hand, that they touched the piece of paper that you now hold.

In my studio, I have a framed invitation to the first Warhol *Campbell's Soup Cans* show out here at Ferus Gallery in 1962. I love the piece, but whenever I show it to people, I find myself saying, "Yeah, but it's a bummer it's not signed." That contradicts my belief that the merit of a piece of art or design should be equal whether or not it was produced by hand or reproduced mechanically; if it's a strong image, it's a strong image.

And yet I am a sucker for the signature. I wish I could know that Warhol touched that invitation.

I never had an autograph book growing up because I grew up in South Carolina, and there was never anyone I wanted an autograph from. But on a regular basis now, I do get autographs from artists and musicians that I like. Ed Ruscha sent me a signed book. Malcolm McLaren signed a bunch of stuff for me. I have records signed by Billy Idol, Alex Van Halen, Henry Rollins, and the guys from Black Sabbath.

I get a lot of flak for my work. Some people don't think I am a very good artist, so when the people I admire come to my studio and leave their signatures, it makes me feel validated in some way, as well. *See, THEY like my art!* It's like when someone would want to sign your yearbook. *Wait, YOU want to sign MY yearbook? You want to leave your name in your own hand in my book?* There is something very intimate about that kind of recognition.

My handwriting is not great. My signature is fairly sloppy. But my mother's handwriting is beautiful, and my grandmother's handwriting was absolutely stunning. My dad's mother is ninety-five, and her handwriting is still beautiful. I used to write letters to people, and in college I studied the correspondence between Sigmund Freud and Wilhelm Fliess. Letter writing was a real art form. It was how you presented your personality and the kind of person you are—through your handwriting. Now it's "C U later" in a text message. The handwritten autograph may remain relevant, but it will be disconnected from that former culture of writing.

Then there is graffiti, the culture that influenced me so much. I never was a traditional graffiti artist, but the premise—to leave your mark where someone else will be forced to see it—has always resonated with me. It is visceral. That thing of writing on stuff: it's saying *I exist*, but also, *I exist in a way that dominates you*. When it comes to graffiti, putting your name up is a dominance thing. Which is why it has often broken down into tribes, crews, gangs where people form alliances. Leaving your name on the wall is a primitive drive—about broadcasting your name and about claiming territory. *I was here and this is mine.*

I think of my art as having a signature, even if it's not signed or stamped with my name or Obey. It has recurring motifs, a visual iconography that becomes recognizable as the overall style of my work. There are so many people out there who are doing amazing things and awful things. It's daunting as an artist to just look at how much is out there and think, *I'm going to make something that is my unique signature, my unique autograph on the world.*

In my late teens, I started to get a grasp on a few things: human psychology, branding, things that worked well as logos, as memorable art, and then how much of a racket it seemed to be for certain people to get attention and to climb to the top of the broadcast pyramid and communicate whatever messages they wanted to the world. I thought, *Well, why shouldn't I do whatever I can to influence how people are thinking?* I maybe did not have the pedigree or authority or connections, but I wanted to go for it.

I wanted to get my messages out and leave my signature.

One of the things I noticed in traditional graffiti was that people who put their signature on the streets more were seen more, and their ideas sunk in more. I understood the power of repetition very quickly. I knew it was important for me to keep putting art in front of people and not deal with gatekeepers and brown-nosing to get gallery shows. Waiting in line was not something I wanted to do. I also realized that merit and power are not based on standardized criteria. But the more something is out there, the more people accept it as valid.

Look at the band DEVO. They had the cones and the hazmat suits. I am attracted to people who have come up with their unique signature for what they do. For a fine artist, that is a style. A Warhol is recognizable. A Monet is recognizable. But we are in a state now—with the internet, and our short attention spans, and the need for instant recognition—that you have to work harder. When I put something up on the wall or on an electrical box in Los Angeles, people in their cars need to be able to see it and process it. It needs to jump out at them.

When I was first looking for places in L.A. to put up my street art, it changed the way I saw the city. I started to see it only as possible places for my work or as places where other people had already left their signatures. Because I think graphically, I have to also pay attention to the visual landscape—to the Norms restaurant sign, the Orpheum Theatre's lettering and marquee—because my work has to have a relationship to what is already there. There was an abandoned theater down the street from the Orpheum, and I remember thinking I should put up a poster above the marquee of that old theater. I wanted to put my art on something that had prestige or remnants of prestige, and that was related to a marquee still in operation down the street. I wanted to be part of that contest for attention.

We know that there have always been people leaving their signatures on walls. Just look at the cave paintings at Lascaux, some of the earliest evidence of humans making artistic markings. The idea of both documenting and mythmaking—you tell your story but with a certain agenda. This is what made humans different from other animals. What changes is how it is perceived, how it is valorized or rejected. When I started my first sticker campaign in Rhode Island, I was arrested a couple times and out on disciplinary probation from my school. Ten years later, I was invited to be part of a museum show called *Rhode Island Treasures*. That's not just about an evolution of my work. It's about changing perceptions.

The value of an autograph depends on who is telling the story, who's got a megaphone, who controls culture. This is why I feel so compelled to persistently insinuate my signature, rather than waiting for people to ask for it. This is why this book matters.

Special-edition Los Angeles Public Library cards designed by Shepard Fairey and Cleon Peterson (left), 2016, and Gajin Fujita, 2019.

GAJIN FUJITA, 2019 • Kidz Gone Bad! Kill Two Succeed

Los Angeles Public Library

Autographs

IN TWO THOUSAND AND NINE
WE LOST A PIECE OF YOURS
AND A PIECE OF MINE.
ON ONE SAD DAY
THE SABER PIECE WAS WIPED AWAY
ON THE BANKS OF THE LA RIVER IT STOOD
- SEEN FROM SPACE IT COULD!
A CLASSIC GRAFF ICON IT WAS
- ONE OF STREET ART'S GREATES LOVES
FAREWELL TO THE MIGHTY SABER
THE SILENT SENTINEL OF
THE LA RIVER

ALDEN WOOD, 2018

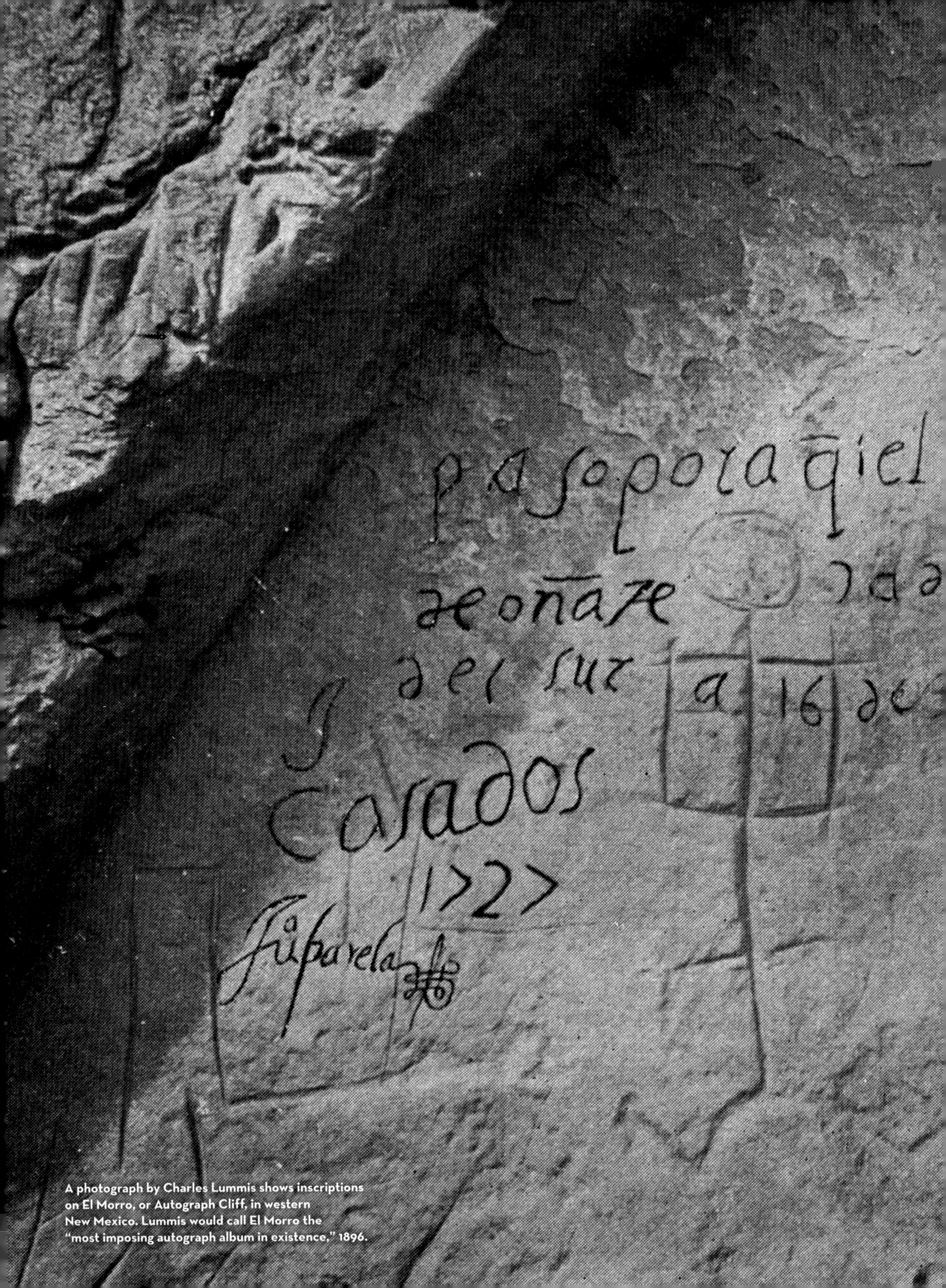

A photograph by Charles Lummis shows inscriptions on El Morro, or Autograph Cliff, in western New Mexico. Lummis would call El Morro the "most imposing autograph album in existence," 1896.

THE AUTOGRAPH BOOK OF L.A.

JOSH KUN

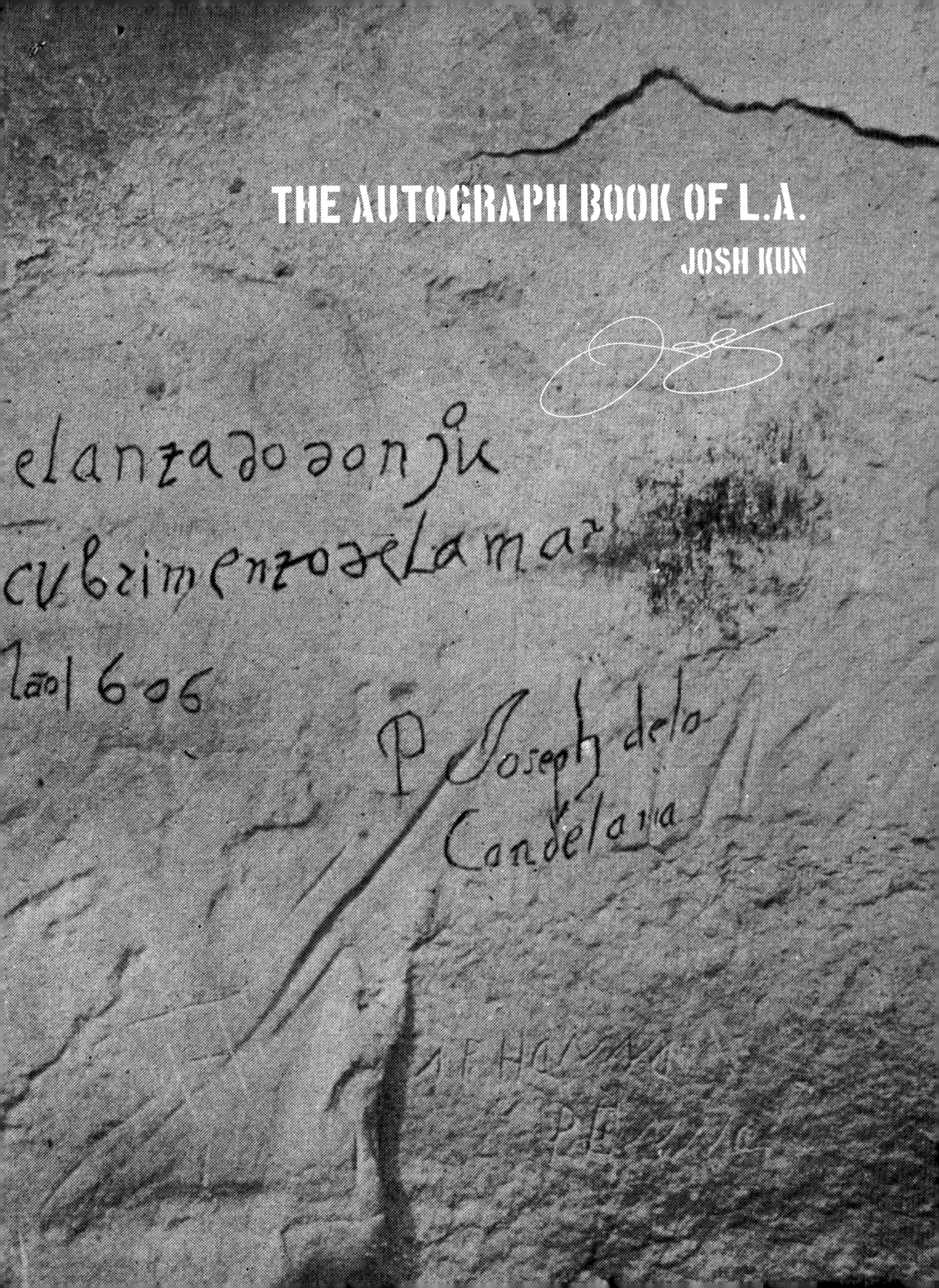

Members of vaudeville group Singer's Midgets sign the world's largest register at the Los Angeles Chamber of Commerce, 1925.

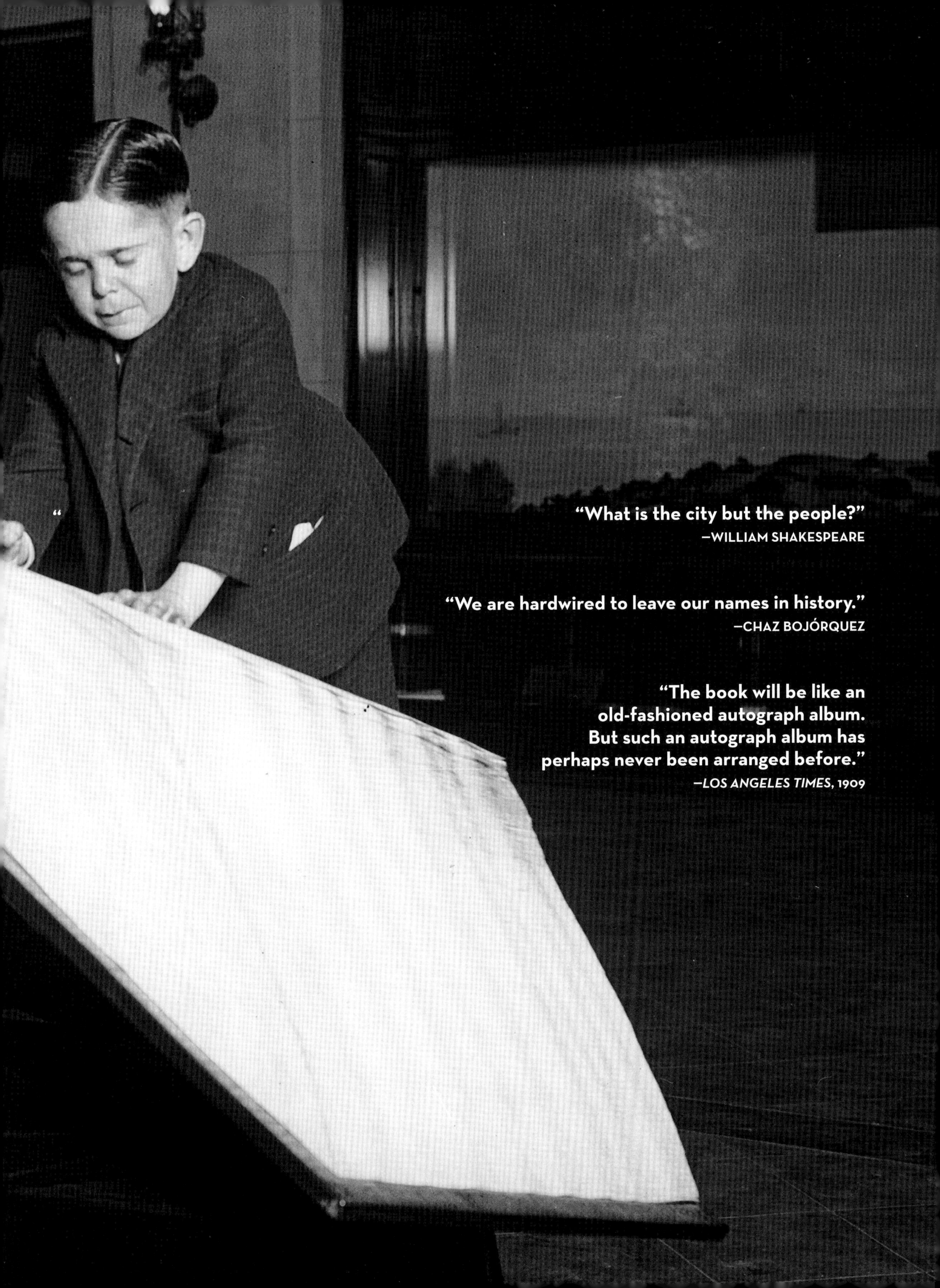

"What is the city but the people?"
—WILLIAM SHAKESPEARE

"We are hardwired to leave our names in history."
—CHAZ BOJÓRQUEZ

"The book will be like an
old-fashioned autograph album.
But such an autograph album has
perhaps never been arranged before."
—*LOS ANGELES TIMES*, 1909

ROLL CALL

BIDDY. AMBROSE. FERNANDO. ANGELYNE. JOHN. CHEECH. JANE. FATHER GREG. NIPSY. WILLIE. CAROLINA. PAPI. ED. BOOKER. GUSTAVO. JUDY. LOUIE. BETYE. ART. LAUREN. MILDRED. FRANK. ATTICA. J GOLD. B+. CUBE. MURRAY. MARY. JACKSON. EVE. HAWKINS #1 BEST BURGER. RAFA. RODNEY. PABLO. AHILAN. AKEELA. JOAN. HORACE. MARISELA. DORIS. FUNKAHUATL. KENDRICK. MAR. OCTAVIA. XOCHI. SHUGGA. ANDERSON. KORLA. LIL PUPPET. EVAN. ROOSEVELT CLASS OF 2019. GRONK. SHOSON. RAMONA. YAMILA. SHIZU. WOLFGANG. ROBIN. ESTEVAN. HADDA. LYNELL. KAMASI. JULIA. MAGIC. RAS G.

YOUR NAME HERE.

THIS ONE'S DEDICATED TO THE ONE I LOVE.

SIGN YOUR NAME ACROSS MY HEART.

I WAS HERE.

SAY HER NAME.

WE OUT HERE.

REMEMBER ME.

ALWAYS AND FOREVER.

PRESENTE.

C/S.

THE HISTORY OF LOS ANGELES
IS THE HISTORY OF AUTOGRAPHS,
THE HISTORY OF THE SIGNATURES
THAT HAVE BEEN LEFT ON ITS PAGES.

THE CITY IS A BOOK,
AN ENCYCLOPEDIC BINDING OF WALLS,
FREEWAYS, BUILDINGS, ARMS, TREES,
SIDEWALKS, BARRACKS, RIVERBEDS,
BATHROOM STALLS, FACES,
AND ROADSIDE ALTARS.

THE CITY IS AN ENDLESS CALLIGRAPHIC SPRAWL:
BROAD AVENUES, AS HÉCTOR TOBAR ONCE WROTE,
LINED WITH CHINESE PICTOGRAPHS
AND ARABIC CALLIGRAPHY AND CYRILLIC,
LONG BOULEVARDS OF SPANISH EÑES.
THE CITY IS A NAMING OPPORTUNITY
WITH GIFTS AT ALL LEVELS ACCEPTED.

ASK THE CITY,
"CAN I HAVE YOUR AUTOGRAPH?"
THE CITY SAYS,
"I'VE ALREADY GIVEN IT TO YOU.
LOOK UP AT THE WALLS.
LOOK DOWN BENEATH YOUR FEET.
CHECK THE TUNNELS.
WALK THE RIVERBEDS.
SCAN THE TREES AND THE BATHROOM WALLS.
READ THE STREET NAMES AND THE PARK NAMES
AND THE FREEWAY NAMES.
CHECK FOR TAGS."

THE CITY SAYS,
"MY PAGES ARE ALWAYS BEING IMPROVED UPON."

LOS ANGELES PUBLIC LIBRARY

DECVS CIVITATIS LVMEN QVE

Los Angeles Public Library

BOARD OF DIRECTORS
ISIDORE B. DOCKWEILER, PRESIDENT
G. M. GIFFEN,
HENRY W. O'MELVENY,
FRED A. HINES,
HENRY M. NEWMARK.

CHAS. F. LUMMIS, LIBRARIAN.

LOS ANGELES, CAL. Jan. 29, 1910.

Mr. Frederic W. Putnam,
Cambridge, Mass.
My dear Mr. Putnam:-

To thousands in this community your name is a household word. Your name "in your own hand" would be a personal favor and privilege to every one of these who count you among the preferred creditors of their minds. You know how the autograph of one who has enriched our thought interests all classes, from children to philosophers.

On behalf of a city noted for cosmopolitanism ~~and culture~~, the Los Angeles Public Library* is making a special "Autograph Archive" of People who Count. It is securing not only the signature but a characteristic page --- from authors, statesmen, and other thinkers, a verse or paragraph of their best work or an original sentiment; from artists a signed sketch. The response already has been most generous. We have over 700 sheets, including many beautiful water-colors.

This is not a private collection for curiosity or pride or money value; it is undertaken by the Library for the benefit of all who read books, and who care for those that write books, and for those about whom books are written. These pages will be bound alphabetically by class, and are exhibited, with frequent change, in a glass case, where they are greatly enjoyed.

May we tax your generosity to "improve" the enclosed page, replace it in the same mailing flat, and post again to me? Gummed and addressed label with postage is enclosed.

Sincerely Yours,
Chas. F. Lummis
Librarian.

*128,000 volumes; 43,000 card-holders; about 15th in size among public libraries in America; 9th in total circulation, (773,000); 1st in per capita circulation (7.5); 2nd in circulation per volume (6.8). City at last U. S. Census 36th in population (102,000 --- now about 19th with 310,000)

Letter from Charles Lummis, requesting an autograph from Frederic W. Putnam, 1910.

INK ON PAPER

IN 1892, AFTER A VISIT TO THE GRAND CANYON, a trip to a petrified forest in Arizona, a trek across the Mojave and around the Salton Sea, and encounters with sacred rattlesnakes, "Mexican witches," and "aboriginal magicians," Charles Fletcher Lummis, sweating in a weathered Stetson hat, knotted neck sash, and desert-crusted corduroy suit, decided that it was the right time to muse about the state of autograph collecting. "I am not so sure about the present generation," Lummis wrote from a remote section of western New Mexico, "but with most young Americans of my day the autograph album was a cherished institution." He waxed nostalgic about flowers pressed dry between pages signed by friends, about Longfellow signing his name so a young Lummis would never forget him.

Friends and heroes reside in the autograph album. Flirtations and wishes dance across its reams.

Lummis's sudden and peculiar lament for the decline of the autograph album, issued in his book of breathless Southwestern mythmaking, *Some Strange Corners of Our Country*, was triggered by where he was standing, beneath the sandstone cliff of El Morro on the grounds of the Zuni pueblo. Centuries earlier, Spanish explorers and colonists had camped there during their quest to take the land, and like graffiti artists bombing a freeway overpass, they left their marks on the walls of the cliff—or, as Lummis put it, "The heroes wrote their autographs upon a vast perpendicular page of stone, with their swords which had won the New World for pens."

In his first rendering of "inscription rock," Lummis lauded autographs as colonialist calligraphy, civilizing scribbles— names written into sand that "were piercing an unknown and frightful wilderness in which no civilized being dwelt." For Lummis, the "autograph cliff" was a landmark of conquest delivered through rugged penmanship, signatures as the frontline against the savagery and barbarism of the Indian desert that he was helping to invent. Of course, the signatures he cherished were written around the rock's first autographs, original Indian pictographs that belong to a long history of indigenous rock art that as far back as 250 AD had left Anasazi and Hohokam petroglyphs depicting prayers, hunts, visions, and clans scraped and scratched onto rocks with basalt stone chisels and hammers (California petroglyphs were first found in Lassen County in the 1850s). The Spanish names of soldiers, governors, and missionaries were scrawled to prove that each of these men *pasó por aqui* (passed by here), as many of them described it. They left names, and they left dates, so there could be no doubt—so that, they hoped, they could never be forgotten.

There are names in English on the autograph cliff as well, but they came later and belong, Lummis surmised, to Saxon vandals. Lummis dubbed the cliff an autograph album, but it was also a reverse prototype of wall writing, gang tags, and murals, a precursor of the Motor Yard, the Estrada Courts, the Venice Pavilion, the Slauson rails, or the Arroyo riverbed. Pueblo Indians got up first. Then the Spaniards tagged on top of them. Then the Anglos tried to cross it all out. No thick-tip markers, no aerosol, no ballpoint missives filling the back pages of a high-school yearbook. Just sand, stone, and signatures on a wall that have always been, and will always be, joined by others.

ANGELYNE, 2018

Four years later, Lummis returned to El Morro to pen another tribute to the same spot, this time for his foundational booster magazine, *The Land of Sunshine*. His anti-Indian sentiment was more subdued the second time around, but the cliff was still mostly a monument to Spanish conquest, for "nowhere else have so many men of historic weight carved their names and dates in stone." Lummis christened it "the most imposing autograph album in existence." What did Lummis love most about El Morro? It was where the names of the powerful had been left, where conquistadores "fell into the way of leaving their names." If Spain's colonization of indigenous America was, as Lummis once put it, "one of the greatest achievements made by man in all his history," then El Morro was its trophy case and Hall of Fame. It cemented for him not only the romance of a skewed settler version of Southwestern history, but the romance of a skewed version of what autographs were for. In New Mexico, the autograph album went from being a place friends could leave memories and dedications to being a model of corralling fame and power, and collecting the calligraphic spoils of history's brutalizing victors.

Seven years before his first visit to El Morro, Lummis had already made his famous "tramp across the continent," a journalistic publicity stunt in which he walked from Ohio to a new job as city editor of the *Los Angeles Times*. He arrived in L.A. as a headline, famous for being famous. He was a nineteenth-century Angelyne, a Kardashian in a Mexican rancher's jacket who knew how to capture people's attention for the things he wanted to promote.

Lummis first honed his self-branding skills as a college student on the East Coast, when he managed to create buzz around his first homemade book of poems—printed by hand on birch bark—by sending it directly to famous poets he wanted to be associated with, like Walt Whitman and Henry Wadsworth Longfellow. The plan worked on Longfellow, who wrote Lummis back with a personalized rave review that Lummis used to market his newfound poetic stature. In Los Angeles, he perfected his formula of courting fame by association when he became editor of *The Land of Sunshine*, a periodical that, before it morphed into *Out West* and *Overland Monthly*, few beyond Southern California knew anything about. He sent copies of the magazine with requests to spread the word (and solicitations to write in future issues) to John Muir, Jack London, Ina Coolbrith, and others with notable bylines.

Lummis's Los Angeles home, El Alisal, soon became the place where all his notable acquaintances were invited to socialize and network in person, to become live actors in his mythical vision of Southern California. As Kevin Starr described it, El Alisal "dramatized perhaps better than anything he had written Lummis's feeling for the rugged romance of Southern California as daughter of New Spain. There, gathering the talent and literati of the day, Lummis would urge them along toward that shimmery Southern California which ever held his imagination." At a series of elaborate, theatrical dinners and parties he famously dubbed "Noises," Lummis gathered together civic leaders, actors, politicians, generals, scientists, intellectuals, painters, and poets—from Muir and Will Rogers to Clarence Darrow to Zitkala-noni, a Sioux survivor of the Battle of Wounded Knee—and asked them all to sign his house guest book. It became Lummis's own portable inscription rock, an L.A. version of El Morro, that kept a record of all who passed through his home. It was, by extension, also a record of his own celebrity, documenting traces of Lummis at the center of a star-studded social circle. His Rolodex of scribbled signatures, sayings, and personal tributes was wielded as proof of his prestige: Lummis mattered.

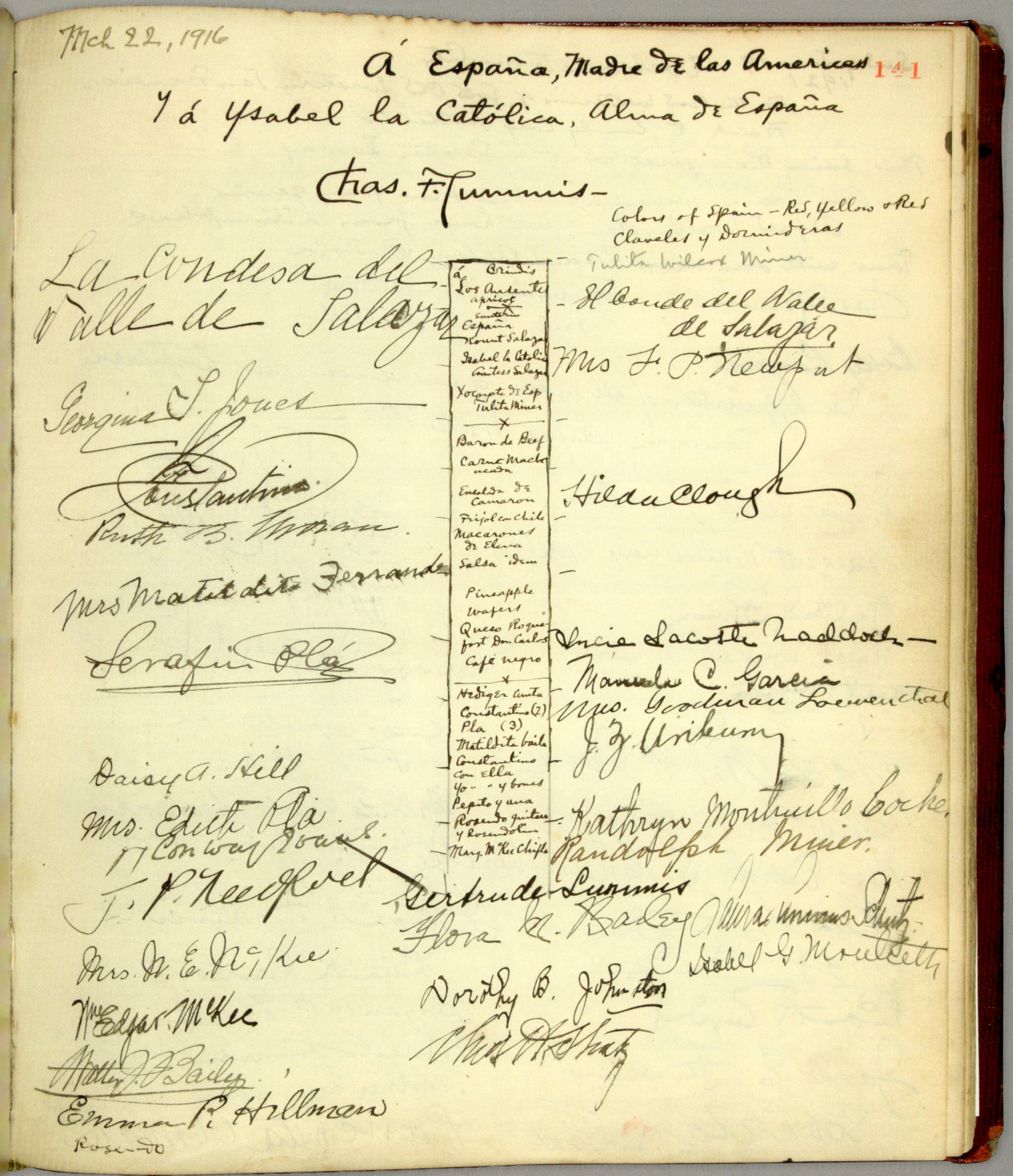
Mch 22, 1916

Á España, Madre de las Americas 141

Y á Ysabel la Católica, Alma de España

Chas. F. Lummis—

Colors of Spain — Red, Yellow & Red
Claveles y Dormideras
Tulita Wilcox Miner

La Condesa del Valle de Salazar

Brindis
á Los Ausentes
apricot
España
Ysabel la Católica
Baron de Beef
Carne Machacada
Ensalada de Camaron
Frijol en Chile
Macarones de Elena
Salsa idem
Pineapple Wafers
Queso Roquefort Don Carlos
Café negro
Constantino (2)
Pla (3)
Matildita baila
Constantino con Ella
Pepito y una
Rosendo guitarra

El Conde del Valle de Salazar
Georgina T. Jones
Constantino
Ruth B. Moran
Hilda Clough
Mrs Matildita Ferrando
Serafin Plá
Lucie Lacoste Maddock
Manuela C. Garcia
Mrs. Goodman Loewenthal
Daisy A. Hill
Mrs. Edith Pla
17 Conway Road
Kathryn Montriello Cocke
Randolph Miner
Gertrude Lummis
Flora M. Bailey
Mrs. W. E. McKee
Wm Edgar McKee
Dorothy B. Johnston
Emma P. Hillman
Rosendo

NOISES SEATING CHART, 1916 • A page from Charles Lummis's housebook details the guests and the menu at a Noises gathering.

Lummis had a kindred contemporary spirit in Austrian writer Stefan Zweig, who also collected notable people as a way of collecting notable signatures. "Many welcome and famous guests visited our house in those years," Zweig recounted of his home in Salzburg where he threw his own Noises. "But even in the hours when I was alone I was surrounded by a magic circle of distinguished figures from the past whose shades and whose traces I had gradually managed to summon." The autographs and drawings left by Lummis's famous guests similarly helped him create his own magic circle of distinguished figures, figures whose shades and traces Lummis would go on to summon whenever he needed them.

And he needed them when, after the controversial and sexist firing of librarian Mary Jones (in what became known as "The Great Library War"), he was appointed city librarian of the Los Angeles Public Library in 1905. "Librarian Lummis Sheds Corduroy; Keeps Old Hat," read the *L.A. Examiner* headline announcing his new position. "Picturesque garb he used to wear gives place to store clothes and stiff collar with tie." There was nothing stiff-collar about Lummis's five-year term as city librarian. Not trained as a librarian, Lummis approached the job with the brash, maverick sensibility he had become notorious for, determined to elevate both the holdings and standing of the Library (then the sixteenth largest public library in the U.S.) and to use the Library to elevate the national standing of Los Angeles (then the twentieth largest city in the U.S.) as a burgeoning cultural center at the farthest edge of the American West. He created an official brand to be engraved in the Library's books, warned patrons of shoddy research by putting "pseudo expert" stickers in volumes he didn't respect, green-lit the construction of a smoking-friendly roof garden reading room, and created a "walking reference desk" that kept librarians mobile. He established the photography collection, the California history collection, and the Spanish history collection, all while racking up a reputation for drinking, smoking, and working from home.

Lummis was an expert booster, and he advertised the Library across the city, targeting factories and schools. He wanted the Library to be a "university of the people" and an "experiment in democracy," an institution that could serve as "a workshop for scholars including every painter's apprentice or working boy or streetcar man who wishes to learn, just as much as it includes the Greek professors or the dilettante." One of his first moves toward this mission was to imagine the autograph album of El Morro taking new shape as the autograph album of Los Angeles Public Library.

WILLIAM HENRY DRAKE, 1907 • "Shere Khan" The wicked Tiger in Rudyard Kipling's *Jungle Book* story "Tiger-Tiger"

The idea first hit him in 1905, after the Library received a donation of a signed holograph manuscript by Wilkie Collins. Soon after, Lummis tested his plan to establish "a system of collecting autographs" with the board. "There are few intelligent people who have not some interest in distinguished autographs," he wrote. "At a very small expense for the stationery, postage, and clerical work, this library could found an autograph department." The collection launched in 1906 with Lummis sending blank, specialty stationery with embossed letterhead—"Los Angeles Public Library Autographs"—to dozens of well-known national politicians, diplomats, generals, zoologists, writers, astrologists, painters, sculptors, and poets. Lummis's solicitation letter identified them all as "People Who Count," people who had a name that was "a household word." He asked them to "improve the enclosed page" and send it back to him with the provided mailing flat—gummed, addressed, and postage paid.

The project received write-ups in the *Los Angeles Times*, and by 1909, Lummis had gathered autographs from "800 celebrities" including Mark Twain, Andrew Carnegie, John Quincy Adams, Jane Addams, the painter Frederic Remington, Lillie Devereaux Blake ("of equal rights fame"), *The Jungle Book* illustrator William H. Drake, and *The Wonderful Wizard of Oz* author L. Frank Baum. Lummis's plan was not to just create the archive and thereby bring people who count into the vaults of the Library, but to use this new register of renown to promote the Library and the city as hubs of fame and excellence. His plan was to publicly broadcast the collection in a series of small exhibitions (which happened) and a bound volume to be kept in a glass case with "one page turned each day" (which did not).

Like so many of Lummis's projects, the Autograph Collection was a mix of preservation and hype, scholarship and spectacle, research and zealous boosterism. It was a way of inventing a Los Angeles that didn't quite exist. L.A. was still a city in search of itself, a "half-horse town" (as Aldous Huxley once said) in the midst of infrastructural change and rapid population growth. Just who constituted the "social polity" of L.A. was up for grabs, and with the Autograph Collection, Lummis was throwing his hat and hundreds of his favorite signatures in the ring.

The collection—which includes signatures, handwritten speeches, watercolors, illustrations, news clippings, and cyanotype portraits photographed by Lummis himself—is a fascinating who's who of the United States during the Gilded Age and Progressive Era. Lummis's taste moves agnostically from sculptors (Julia Bracken Wendt, Emilie Stearns Perry) to political firebrands (Belva Ann Lockwood, Eugene V. Debs), from activists (Samuel Gompers, Jane Addams) to writers (Charles W. Chestnutt, Ambrose Bierce, L. Frank Baum). Contributions from popular songwriter Charles K. Harris, "America the Beautiful" lyricist Katharine Lee Bates, and Spanish violin virtuoso Marie Azpiroz exist alongside submissions from pioneering feminist writer Charlotte Perkins Gilman and influential African American educator Booker T. Washington. Subsequent attempts to extend Lummis's original collection kept its intellectual and cultural diversity alive with contributions from Langston Hughes, Carlos Bulosan, Arna Bontemps, Helen Keller, and Isaac Asimov, to name but a few.

A booth at the Los Angeles County Fair advertises its graphology services, 1937.

Lummis's interest in the importance of autographs as tools for measuring social value and documenting cultural capital was very much a product of his time. By the nineteenth century, autograph collecting in the U.S. was all the rage as a popular hobby, and individualized autograph books joined scrapbooks and memory books in a new vernacular culture of homegrown collecting (design historian Jessica Helfand has called scrapbooks "the original open-source technology"). But unlike the inherent populism of scrapbooks, autograph books were also an established practice of elite collectors who helped create a market that attached monetary value to famous signatures. As early as 1815, William B. Sprague had emerged as the nation's most prominent collector. Throughout the century, collecting autographs of people who had "risen above the common herd" grew into an established tradition, with the first autograph-and-rare-manuscript shop in the country opening in New York in 1887.

The autograph craze was fueled by the nineteenth-century interest in the cult of individuality, the belief that cultivating and celebrating individualism was crucial to holding off the rise of the machine and the automation of social life that many, including Lummis, worried would be the result of industrialization. Autographs were "talismans of individuality," as Tamara Plakins Thornton put it, as intimate a personal trace as a lock of hair.

Early American advocates of the power of the autograph included Edgar Allan Poe, who believed that signatures were clues to "mental features." His 1841 essays for *Graham's Magazine*, later collected as "A Chapter on Autography," examined more than seventy autographs from his distinguished literary contemporaries, such as Ralph Waldo Emerson, Washington Irving, and James Fenimore Cooper. Two of Lummis's autograph subjects—John Quincy Adams and Henry Wadsworth Longfellow—were collected and analyzed by Poe. Of the former, Poe remarked that the ex-president's signature was "remarkable for a certain steadiness of purpose pervading the whole." Longfellow's signature exhibited "plain indications of the force, vigor, and glowing richness of his literary style." Such observations were typical of the graphology movement—the study of handwriting as an access route to soul, personality, and character—which Poe was enthusiastically a part of and which had been growing in legitimacy since the early 1800s. The first full-length study of handwriting analysis, Edouard Hocquart's *The Art of Judging the Mind and Character of Men and Women from their Handwriting*, appeared in France in 1812. By the 1830s, the idea that someone's autograph could reveal inner life, as well as nationality, gender, family, and profession, had become commonplace in the United States.

Lummis was not much of a graphologist, though. He was less interested in analyzing autographs for their internal meaning as he was in collecting them for their prestige. For Lummis, the point of the autograph was not to reveal the soul of the signee, but to showcase the power and renown of the collector. By creating the Library's Autograph Collection, Lummis was trying to make a statement about whose names mattered to this young city in the making. If he gathered the signatures of enough People Who Count, maybe he too was someone who counted; maybe the Library was worth paying attention to; maybe L.A. was a city that, someday, would be a household word.

Los Angeles Public Library

Autographs

Taco 'bout Good! Since 1976...

Socorro Herrera
(MAMA YUCA'S)

We love you!!!
Susie Low

Soy la nieta de Mama Yucas y amo su comida y a ella.
Alejandra Treinen

Life after Yuca's opened was so tasty.
[illegible]

Love My Family
[illegible]

WHAT A JOURNEY.
THE BEST FOOD, AND THE BEST FAMILY
MUCH LOVE!
FRED FEDAL

SONIA MEDRANO.
Soy. una delas.
Famosas cosineras.
Y orguyosa de perteneser. a la compañia.
YUCA'S.

MAMA YUCA'S,
FAMOUS YUCATAN FOOD FROM MY SISTER COMES TO LOS ANGELES MADE WITH FLAVOR AND Love THAT OUR MOTHER TAUGHT US!
OPEN 4/1/1976!
LOVE YOU SIS!
PILAR ♡

YUCA'S, 2018

His interest in the autography of the illustrious unwittingly opened up broader questions. Whose names *do* matter? Who deserves to be counted? Who will be remembered? The Autograph Collection became an early entry in a genealogy of marking that shaped the city for the rest of the century. In the university of the people, whose voices are heard? On the pages of the city, whose signatures are valued the most? As one L.A. high-school autograph book put it in 1955, is it the signatures of "the famous" or the "not so famous"?

The autograph is not the gateway to the soul. The autograph is the gateway to the politics of memory, which can be as violent and brutal as claiming an old world as new, as violent and brutal as telling someone that the name written in their own hand is only worth forgetting.

In June of 2018, I worked with City Librarian John Szabo and the Library Foundation of Los Angeles to temporarily re-launch Lummis's autograph collection with a new perspective. In keeping with the spirit of the original archive, we sent blank stationery—a replica of the original, printed by L.A.'s longest-running letterpress, Aardvark Letterpress—to an assortment of contemporary Angelenos (artists, writers, scientists, activists, entertainers, thought leaders), some of whom have operated in the shadows of the spotlight. Famed television producer Norman Lear left a maxim, and famed famous-person Angelyne left a lipstick kiss, but playwright and performer Richard Montoya used his autograph to offer a tribute to Ralph Lazo, the Mexican American teenager who in 1942 volunteered to be interned at Manzanar alongside his Japanese American friends as an act of solidarity. "Tongva women have never left their land," Tongva elder Julia Bogany wrote on her autograph page, "They just became invisible."

But we also flipped the original collection on its head and provided blank stationery at branch libraries across the city with an open invitation for all to leave their mark. The People Who Count were now everyday Angelenos, writing their names, representing their streets and communities, and telling their stories in their own hand. Jeremy Ruiz, a senior at Locke High School, wrote down how tired he was because of the eight projects due for his classes. The Stitchin' Sistahz Quilt Circle listed their members and spelled out their textile mission, and the Skid Row artist Shugga left a signature. There are renderings of the Chinatown Branch Library, a "Dario Was Here" tag, a list of "Things That Remind Me of Highland Park," and a drawing by three-and-a-half-year-old Abby Sanchez. An LAPD officer signed his stationery with "Lemme See Your Hands," and Esto One sketched an L.A. skyline of liquor stores and LAPD helicopters. The family behind Yuca's taco hut—the Loz Feliz institution that opened in 1976—left a page full of memories and a photograph of the restaurant's founder, "Mama" Socorro Herrera. Michael Castellanos left a different kind of roll call: a crayon memorial to Trayvon Martin, Eric Garland, Oscar Grant, "and all of the victims of unlawful, unjustified police shootings." David Gurnick of Chatsworth signed his name with a single hope: "I would just like to be part of it."

This autographic inversion had some precedence. In 1925, the L.A. Chamber of Commerce created a massive, supersized Visitor's Registry Book and invited all visitors to their headquarters to sign it. Dubbing it "The World's Largest Register," the chamber used it as a publicity stunt and invited the vaudeville group Singer's Midgets—most famous for their appearance in *The Wizard of Oz*—to sign it for the cameras. More earnest in its efforts to create a democracy of signatures was the KLAC radio promotion launched to coincide with the 1969 mission of *Apollo 11*. Billing the project as "A Tribute to the Crew of *Apollo 11*," KLAC assembled a large scrapbook of more than a half million cut-and-pasted signatures—in English, Mandarin, and Spanish—from people across Los Angeles as "a public service." Many of them were turned in by entire elementary school classrooms and entire neighborhoods, some by individual city blocks. They are all roughly glued together by hand into a smudged patchwork of paper and ink to create a gigantic DIY calligraphic collage of L.A. names.

The majority of the *Apollo 11* signatures are modest in scale, fighting for attention in teetering columns of cursive. One man, however, did not want to risk that his signature would be overlooked. Robert Ybarra wrote his name three times the size of those around it; he puffed up the squared letters of his name into reinforced, triple-beamed pillars. Like monuments. Like lampposts.

Above it he wrote, "I'll never make it, so I'll make it big."

ROBERT YBARRA, 1969: From "A Tribute to the Crew of *Apollo 11*" (see page 110).

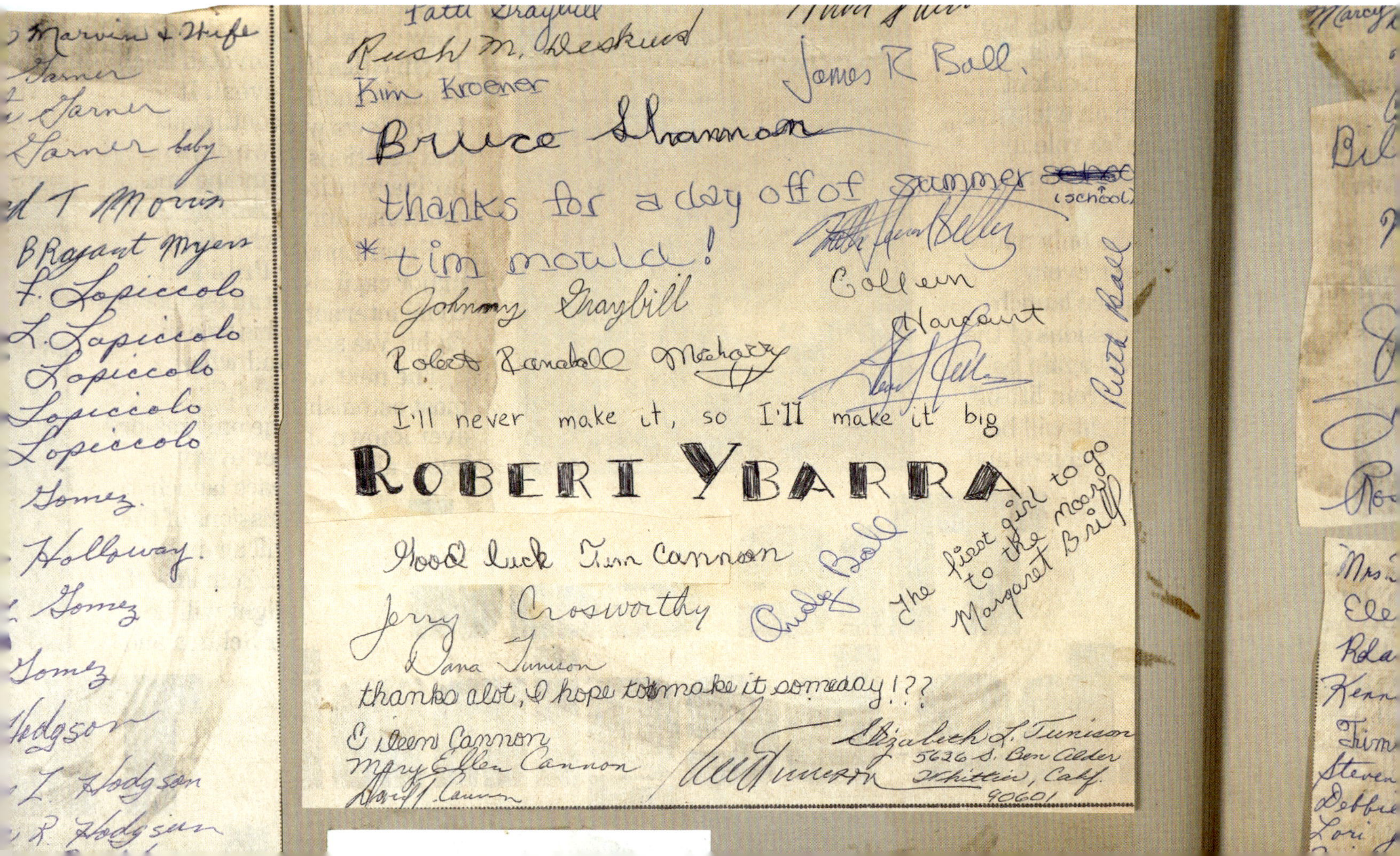

HANDS ON CONCRETE

"TO JOSH, A FUTURE DODGER." Tommy Lasorda signed a picture of himself for me when I was in fourth grade. It didn't fit in my index-card-sized autograph book with brown plastic covers and fake gold "Autographs" lettering, but I kept it close to me anyway, and it quickly became my favorite of the few autographs I already treasured. That is, until a few years later, when I went to a record fair at the Century Plaza Hotel—keynote speaker: Anita Baker—and got the autograph of rapper Egyptian Lover. He signed his 12-inch LP single of "Egypt, Egypt" with a black Sharpie and immediately beat Lasorda at the dedication game: "To Josh, Boom Homeboy." I've had the album framed ever since, and it's now hanging in my office, right next to an LP once owned by my late grandfather, signed and dedicated to him by his version of Egyptian Lover, Ray Conniff ("To Mort, With my sincere thanks, happy listenin"). I never framed the Lasorda photo, probably because I knew that I would never be a Dodger in any future, but a Boom Homeboy? I still hold out for that. There have been stray autographs I've collected since—Spanish pop star Mona Belle, Barry "Greg Brady" Williams—but Egyptian Lover's autograph still lights me up whenever I see it. It places me in time. It manifests my tastes. It reminds me who I've been and how I've wanted to be. People collect celebrity autographs for all sorts of reasons, but this is surely one of them: a name written in someone else's hand gives us a piece of ourselves. So we hunt for them. We become hounds. We hunt and hound for ourselves.

Actress Joan Crawford gives an autograph to a soldier at the Hollywood Canteen, 1943.

EARL CAR
INCLUDES LAVISH REV
Andy
Herbert Marshall
Frank Morgan
Errol Flynn
Jimmy Wallington
Boris Karloff
George Murphy
Charlie Ruggles 1941
Ingrid Bergman
Cordially Walter Pidgeon
Robert Taylor
William Powell
Carole Lombard
Howdy — Gary Cooper
Bette Davis
Greetings
Blessings
Bing

"No autograph hounds allowed" are the first words we see in Disney's 1939 animated film *The Autograph Hound*, which follows Donald Duck, a "web-footed autograph hound," as he sneaks onto the Walt Disney Studios lot in search of celebrity signatures. Clutching his autograph book and crashing dressing rooms and soundstages like a feathered nascent paparazzo, Donald stalks Mickey Rooney (who leaves his signature and then makes it disappear), ice-skating star Sonja Henie (who etches her autograph in ice), comedy trio the Ritz Brothers (they sign Donald's plumed backside), and Shirley Temple (who dots her "i" with a kiss). It's Temple who realizes that this autograph hound is a star in his own right, pulls out her own autograph book, and asks for *his* signature. The hound becomes the hounded, as a circus of celebrities—Clark Gable, Greta Garbo, Groucho Marx, Joan Crawford, among others—leave Donald drowning in a mountain of autograph books awaiting his web-footed signature.

By 1939, the culture of the autograph had already become a standard feature of Hollywood's Golden Age and a key building block of its "Realm of Pretense." A year earlier, Earl Carroll's lavish Sunset Boulevard supper club and theater—an "entertainment palace" replete with a stage with a water curtain, hidden elevator, and revolving tower of four pianos—built the celebrity autograph into its architecture. Gordon B. Kaufmann, the architect responsible for the look of Santa Anita Park and Hoover Dam, made one entire exterior wall of the theater into a "Wall of Fame" with more than one hundred concrete blocks autographed by Hollywood luminaries. The theater's concrete autograph book was an ode to the original concrete autograph book on the grounds of Grauman's Chinese Theatre. When it opened in 1927 as one of young Hollywood's premier celluloid cathedrals, Sid Grauman began asking his famous guests to leave their footprints—and eventually their handprints, handwriting, and in the case of Al Jolson, "knee prints"—in the fresh, wet-pavement blocks of the theater's forecourt.

Leaving your mark in Grauman's forecourt became a Hollywood rite of passage and the ultimate stamp of celebrity authenticity. When it appeared as Khan's Persian Palace in Nathanael West's classic Hollywood novel *The Day of the Locust* (published the same year as *The Autograph Hound*'s release), the theater became the gory chaotic site of fame's underbelly—its corruptions, disillusions, and deceits. In the novel's final scene, a glamorous film premiere erupts into a brutal, terrifying fan riot, with hundreds of feverish autograph seekers (the novel's frustrated screenwriter protagonist Tod Hackett keeps an autographed picture of his obsession, aspiring actress Faye Greener, over his bed) turning on each other in a swirl of panic and violence. West may have even hinted at a connection between the "dream dumps" of Hollywood's fame factory and Charles Lummis's earlier booster experiments with autographs and fame to sell the dream of Los Angeles. He made one character, Earle Shoop, a corduroy-and-Stetson-wearing faux cowboy who works at a saddlery store on Sunset, and maybe even nodded to Lummis when he named the monstrous fame-seeking eight-year-old child actor Adore Loomis.

^ Celebrity signatures hang on the exterior of the Earl Carroll Theatre in Hollywood, among them Robert Taylor, Carole Lombard, and Ingrid Bergman, 1948.

‹ Frank Sinatra signs in concrete outside Grauman's Chinese Theatre in Hollywood, 1965.

YAMILA KUN, 2019

In his 2015 series *Concrete Couples*, the artist John Baldessari used the Grauman's concrete autographs to upend the hierarchies of fame. In a series of nine faux-concrete squares, Baldessari wrote the names of famous couples—Frida and Diego, Romeo and Juliet, Mickey and Minnie—but instead of following the Grauman's autograph formula, he turned them all into mundane lovelorn teenagers etching their names in trees.

The big-screen celluloid star factory of Hollywood threw a wrench into the history of autographs. Before Hollywood, the frenzy of American autograph collecting was predominantly a literary affair. The rise of the autograph in the nineteenth century was linked to the fame of literary heroes like James Fenimore Cooper and Washington Irving, whose signatures became sought-after bounties by a new breed of collectors whom Irving derided as "the mosquitoes of literature" and Walt Whitman pathologized as diseased "autograph monsters." The literary mosquito and the Hollywood mosquito were both modern manifestations of a tradition of collecting famous signatures that dates back to Ancient Greece. Aristotle was an autograph hound (with a penchant for signed maps and manuscripts), as was Ptolemy I. Before its destruction in 48 BCE, the Library of Alexandria was loaded with more than 700,000 manuscripts from across Assyria, Greece, Persia, Egypt, and India, many of them signed by their authors. The tradition flourished in the Renaissance, when the first autograph albums began to appear. Known as *alba amicorum*—"book of friends," "friendship books"—they were bound social-media platforms for sixteenth-century scholars, students, and artists who collected signatures of acquaintances and colleagues.

In twentieth-century America, that tradition most directly lived on in student autograph books and the mad end-of-the-year rush to have friends sign for posterity. "School Day Memories Bring Back Pleasant Thoughts of Happy Hours Spent in Work and Play," reads the title page of the L.A. high-school autograph book of Edna Frouein. From 1929 to 1933, she filled the book with messages and notes from her classmates. "Dear Edna, remember me in Spanish and how smart we both were," one "palsy-walsy" wrote. "When you are old and live by the sea," another wrote, "Put on your speck and come to see me." The goal of these autograph books was to collect the signatures of the known and the familiar, to mark a period in time, to inscribe names and memories before they were forgotten.

But the autograph hounds of Hollywood, and the economy of celebrity signatures that they gave birth to, kept the autograph away from the everyday and within the realm of stardom, where Charles Lummis liked it best. For Lummis, the ultimate job of the autograph was to be a trace of the famous. Sure, it could afford some personal solace and satisfaction and maybe even beef up the contours of recollection, but ultimately it was handy for bragging rights. Lummis's hope was that the cultural value of an autograph could inflate the cultural value of its recipient: *I may not be a star, but I am star adjacent.*

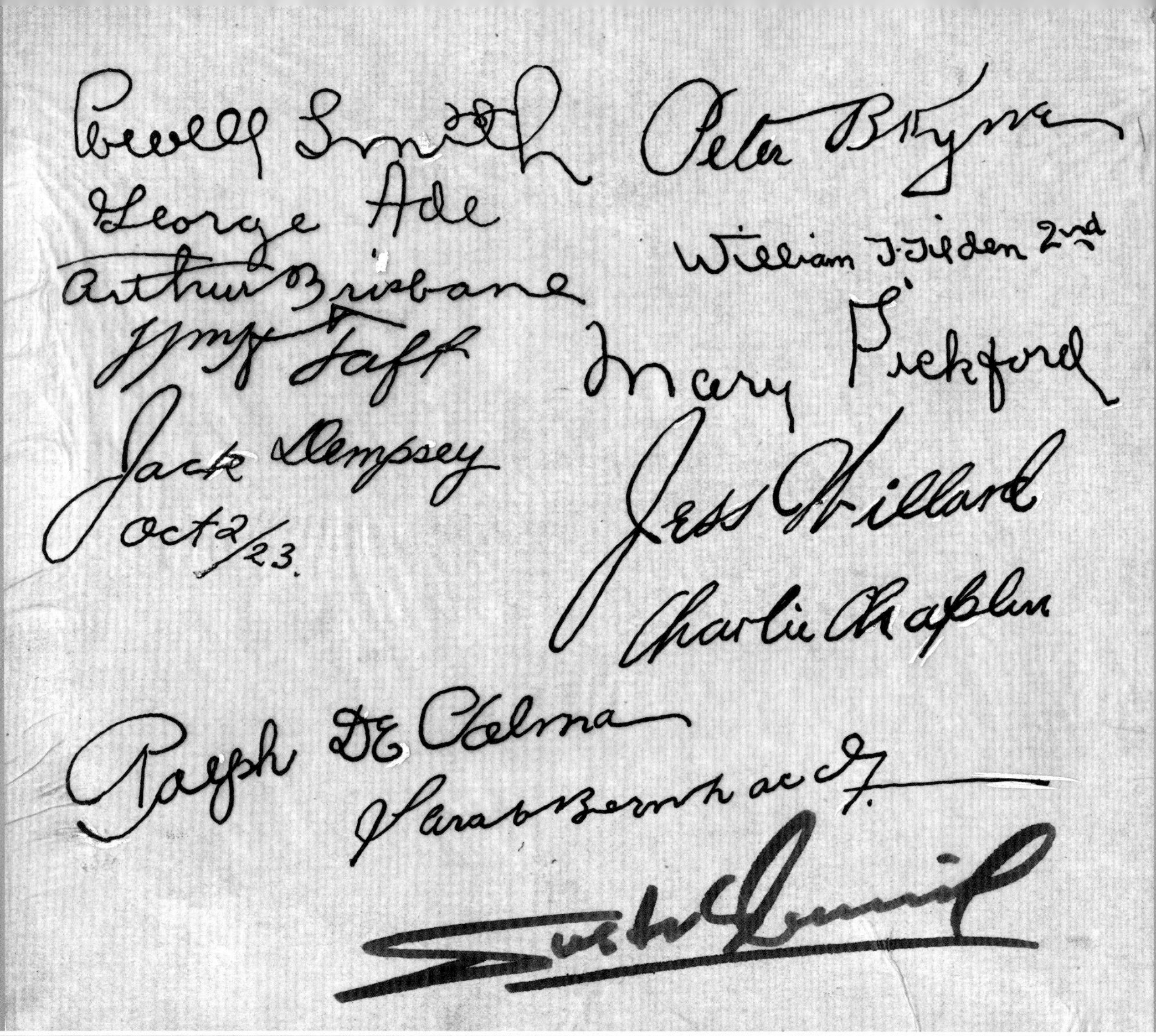
Peter B. Kyne
George Ade
William T. Tilden 2nd
Arthur Brisbane
Wm H Taft
Mary Pickford
Jack Dempsey
Oct 2/23.
Jess Willard
Charlie Chaplin
Ralph DePalma
Sarah Bernhardt.

6230
REET CLOSED
REAU OF ENGINEERS
BarBara Stanwyck
Howdy —
Gary Cooper
Tyrone Power
Kindest Ever —
Ginger Rogers
Best wishes
from
Clark Gable

Ever since the first silent shorts were projected onto theater screens in 1910, the autograph has been Hollywood currency, living squarely in the domain of mediated celebrity. The autograph hunter became a constant, mostly unwanted, extra—stalking stars for an inky touch of their hand, lurking at stage doors, screaming in bleachers, and crowding roped-off premiere lines. *Our Gang* featured an "autograph seeker" character in 1936, and Betty Brewer played an "autograph hound" in 1944's *Cover Girl*. With the advent of film, radio, and eventually television, the autograph was forever linked to an industry and culture of fame; a screen, stage, and airwaves galaxy of stars—the spectacular apex of what scholar Leo Braudy notably chronicled as the "frenzy of renown."

Hollywood autograph hunters became famous, and infamous, in their own right. Joe Ackerman came to Hollywood in 1941 and started grabbing signatures wherever he could—at Ciro's, the Mocambo, and Slapsie Maxie's, at stage entrances on NBC and CBS lots, at the gates of Columbia and Paramount, at premieres at Grauman's and the Egyptian. His autograph collection is still on display in Hollywood, behind glass in a museum that was once Max Factor's makeup studio (Factor once had his own guest book as well as an autograph book signed by all the stars who came through his doors). Ackerman was "Hollywood's beloved autograph hound," but these days autograph hounds are at best tolerated and at worst reviled as "celebrity plankton." The Twitter bio for Mike Medlin, one of the more notoriously aggressive and persistent Sharpie-bearing collectors of this century, reads more like a gangster's boast: "gettin' graphs and takin' names in Hollywood, CA." Instead of autograph books, modern-day professional collectors patrol the streets of Los Angeles in SUVs loaded with photographs; stake out restaurants, nightclubs, and conventions; and then flip as many signed 11 × 14s as they can on eBay.

Implied in that now-age-old question, "May I have your autograph?" is an understood transaction. There is the assumption and recognition that the *you* being asked is a *you* that matters, and that the *you* doing the asking will be enriched—spiritually, emotionally, financially—by having a signature on a page that could come from only one hand, or by a dedication to you in your own name that changes a photograph or a book from a cold, anonymous object into a personalized gift. The autograph is also the premise for a dream: maybe, like that web-footed autograph hound of 1939, the autograph hunter will become the autograph hunted; maybe the autograph will double as a magical transfer of renown, and by receiving the signature, one day you will be the one doing the signing.

That's a dream Los Angeles is built on.

^ Signatures from the register of the Alexandria Hotel in downtown Los Angeles, including Jack Dempsey, Mary Pickford, and Charlie Chaplin, 1934.

‹ Earl Carroll and chorus girls from his Earl Carroll Theatre pose with celebrity autographs etched in concrete blocks. The signatures typically hung outside of the building, 1940.

"Love to you all." A note from actress Shirley Temple, six years old in 1935, when she left her handprints in the forecourt of Grauman's Chinese Theatre, Hollywood, 1938.

Students hand-write Chinese characters on a blackboard. "Doesn't a lifetime feel like one year?" writes the girl on the left. "The spring breeze is warm and gentle. The grass is sprouting up. In ancient time, my homeland..." the boy marks on the right. Translation by Sulafa Zidani.

Names are carved into the wooden doors at Drum Barracks, a military outpost near the Port of Los Angeles, that was used during the American Civil War.

ACRYLIC ON CONCRETE

THE EARLIEST KNOWN EVIDENCE of a human signature is by Gar Ama on the back of a Sumerian clay tablet in 3100 BC. The Brazilian artist Vik Muniz describes its impact like this:

> *Unconsciously, with his mark, [he] adjusted the historical role of the individual from being a description or a character to become a flesh and blood living person who could manifest himself, a sworn-in protagonist. After the advent of the signature . . . the simplest form of assuring a legacy became leaving a mark, a personal one, something that would become indelible by habit and religion, something unique, easily identified and yet inimitable and pure, as it would combine in equal proportion the gesture of the body and the intention of the spirit.*

It's hard to say for sure, but it's likely that the earliest surviving evidence of a signature left on the built environment of Los Angeles can be glimpsed in a faded 1873 black-and-white photograph in the collection of the Central Library. The name is barely noticeable in the image of the grated cell doors of the Drum Barracks in Wilmington—a Union army headquarters during the Civil War—but it's there, split down the middle between the cracked open door and its upper frame. Maybe a soldier left it there, maybe tall enough to reach, maybe helped up by a stool or a tree stump or a friendly boost, determined to make sure others knew he was there by leaving a scrawl—first name that begins with a C, last name with an H—in dark grease paint, or by etching it into the wood with a sharpened blade. As anthropologist Susan A. Phillips has documented, the barracks' nearby powder magazine is the real signature gold mine, its walls covered in inscribed names, including William S. Banning, the son of Wilmington godfather Phineas Banning, who also founded the Port of Los Angeles.

In Phillips's many studies of L.A. as an archive of urban vernacular expression, the next markings of note start to arrive in the early 1900s, when hobos traveled up and down the L.A. River and made camp in Griffith Park. In August of 1914, hobo alphabet inventor Ray Livingston etched his hobo moniker "A-No.1" into a concrete wall under a river bridge. He left symbols as directions for heading up river to the park and signed his name next to two fellow vagabond travelers: Oakland Red and Tucson Kid. In the 1920s, patrons of the downtown speakeasy in the basement of the King Edward Hotel left their names on the bathroom walls. As sidewalks proliferated in the post-World War I construction boom, so did the tradition of Angelenos leaving their names in wet concrete. The total result is a boundless urban inventory of names, of indexical traces of selves rendered in writing—the auto/self of the graph, the graph produced by the self/auto—that reveal the city as a registry of what geographer Doreen Massey once called "throwntogetherness," its dynamic state of constant difference and co-presence. These etched and carved and inked and sprayed names were all thrown up to fight against erasure. "If mortality defines the human condition," Phillips writes in the afterword to this book, "then the signature outlasts it."

A piece by Phantom Street Artist in a Santa Monica tunnel, 1992.

The autograph's fight against mortality puts it in locked arms with all hieroglyphs, with all words, written and symbolic effigies that survive the things they describe. "Words begin as description," as Susan Brind Morrow once explained in her studies of Egyptian hieroglyphics and pyramid texts. "They are prismatic vehicles of hidden, deeper shades of thought. You can hold them up at different angles until the light bursts through an unexpected color. The word carries the living thing concealed across millennia." Which is why whose words are seen, whose names are erased, whose autographs are collected, can matter so much. Which is why names are political. Which is why memory is never fair. Because words and names are not words and names. They are vessels that carry the bodies and lives embedded within them forward in time. They are statements of presence and wishes for endurance, reminders that those who came before cannot so easily be made to disappear.

Which is also why graffiti is seen as destructive, or as empowering. Earlier, I referred to the signed walls and pavements of the Grauman's Chinese and Earl Carroll theaters as concrete autograph books. But I should have clarified. They are *sanctioned* concrete autograph books. The city is full of autograph books carved in concrete, cut in wood, spray-painted on brick, marked in steel, that are unsanctioned, guerrilla, and subversive—direct on-the-run and on-the-fly hits on the autograph's built-in power play. The *graph* of autograph comes from the same *graf* as graffiti, from the Greek *grapho*, or scratch. Writing on the walls of the city has long been a practice for the un-autographed, those whose names were erased and ignored by design. And in this "thirty-five-mile-per-hour" city where privacy and privatization have been urban religions, where we shuttle alone between cars and homes, where public spaces are endangered species and cameras replace doorbells and gated yards fill gated communities, broadcasting messages in public is an especially radical act.

Leaving your name on a wall—whether in wild-style balloons or wheat-pasted posters or dripping tags or slicing gang cross-outs—is also leaving an autograph nobody asked for. It is a demand for recognition; a request for a public reckoning with your presence. The battle for recognition inherent in all street and wall autographs is just one example of what the band Rage Against the Machine once called *The Battle of Los Angeles*—a centuries-long battle over land, housing, rights, power, and memory. For the cover of their album bearing that title, it's no coincidence the band chose to spell it out in original artwork by Phantom Street Artist, known for his all-city, spray-painted, body-bag silhouettes that speak from the dead: "These Are Thoughts That Set Fire To Your City," "Art Saves Lives," "United Snakes of America."

Most histories of graffiti, murals, and gang tags in L.A.—from the tar, smoke, and felt-tip marker days to the days after the wide release of aerosol cans in the 1940s—frame wall writing and street art as weapons in the struggle over the "right to the city," the struggle over place, territory, and belonging. When "the places associated with people who have limited power are more likely to be destroyed," who has the right to the city? Whose rights matter more than others? Whose names should be on the wall, on the street name, on the freeway sign? Whose city is it?

SOLDIER
TLES ARE NOT WON BY ARMS ALONE
RE MUST EXIST ABOVE ALL ELSE A
RITUAL IMPULSE—A WILL TO VICTORY.
WAR THERE CAN BE NO SUBSTITUTE
FOR VICTORY"
STATESMAN
"COULD I HAVE BUT A LINE A CENTURY
HENCE CREDITING A CONTRIBUTION TO
THE ADVANCE OF PEACE, I WOULD GLADLY
YIELD EVERY HONOR WHICH HAS BEEN
ACCORDED BY WAR"
A DAMIAN
GARCIA PARK
VIVA, LA REVOLUCIN

לשמוע אל הרנה ואל התפלה
HIGH HOLIDAY SERVICES
ראש השנה
ROSH HASHONA
Thur. & Fri. Sept. 8th 9th
יום כפור
YOM KIPPUR
סוכות
SUCCOTH
סליחות
SLICHOTH
דרשות
BY Rabbi MORDECAI AARON GANZWEIG
חזן
MAKE YOUR RESERVATIONS NOW!
FROM 10 to 6 P.M. STARTING
TO RESERVE SEATS CALL 262-3922
262-7413 262-8224

We can see these struggles unfold in photographs throughout the Library's collection. Built atop original Tongva swampland, Westlake Park was renamed MacArthur Park in 1942 to honor General Douglas MacArthur. The new name came with a new lakeside structure, a statue and memorial wall dedicated to the vaunted World War II figure. In 1983, members of the Revolutionary Communist Party, who had already used the park as a protest and demonstration site during International Workers Day, petitioned the City to change the park's name to pay tribute to Damien Garcia—a party member who, three years earlier, had been killed during a May Day rally in East Los Angeles. (While the official account attributed his death to gang violence, some believed he was murdered for his role in hoisting the RCP flag atop the Alamo, tearing down the Texas flag, and calling out Anglo Texans for "sucking the blood of the Chicano people.") In an uncredited photo, it's clear that the biggest signature on their petition was the one they left on the MacArthur memorial itself, spray-painting the new name of the park on both sides of the statue and providing a subversive aerosol subhead to the late general's own dictum engraved above it in stone: "Battles are not won by arms alone."

Or there are Gary Leonard's photographs of the Breed Street Shul in Boyle Heights. Originally a pillar of the neighborhood's thriving Jewish community (once the largest in Los Angeles), the home of the Talmud Torah congregation eventually fell into disrepair after the majority of eastside Jews headed west in the 1950s. After services at the *shul* formally ceased in the 1990s, the writing started to go up: gang tags and graffiti covered the walls of worship, filling the emptied building with dense layers of names, slogans, and affiliations. While many decried the *shul*'s new signatories as vandals defacing a historic landmark, their writing was a clear testament to transformations of place in Boyle Heights (freeway construction, urban renewal campaigns) and to histories of urban change (migrations in, migrations out). In one of Leonard's photographs, the Hebrew letters of a fallen High Holiday services sign share the frame with the Gothic letters of Chicano graffiti. Like so many other abandoned structures in the city's history—the old KEHE/KFI broadcast studios, for example, or the legendary Golden Gate Theatre—the Breed Street Shul became its own living autograph book, full of the hieroglyphics of neighborhood change that, in the words of critic and theorist Norman Klein, make L.A. "a collection of micro-climates, of ethnicity, and layers of urban traces, one upon the other."

^ "Viva Damian Garcia Park!" Communist activists attempted to rename MacArthur Park, which takes its name from World War II General Douglas MacArthur. They hoped to honor murdered Revolutionary Communist Party member Damian Garcia, 1983.

‹ A sign marking High Holiday Services lies in the graffitied Talmud Torah Synagogue of Boyle Heights, 1995.

Once you start looking for them, they are everywhere—layerings of history, palimpsests of signatures, pentimenti of autographs, sediments of names. The faded "Frank's" logo on the side of the building that used to house Frank's Camera in Highland Park with a fresh, full-color tag beneath it as a post-gentrification subtitle. The grid of newly settled bricks near Alameda and Industrial Streets, each etched in chalk or marker with angled and curvaceous nicknames (*L.A. Times* critic Carolina Miranda dubbed them "contemporary *placas*" when she posted a photo of them on Instagram). An off-ramp electrical pole covered in a layer of tags that are covered with stapled flyers for a cumbia concert at Salon Lazaros, a fumigation company promising to get rid of bed bugs and termites, and someone who buys homes with "fast cash." The Crenshaw mural of the Black Panthers that was hit with a blanket of swastikas. The downtown-parking-lot, eighty-foot wide, and eighty-five-foot-high blazing East Los Streetscapers mural *El Nuevo Fuego*, now captioned with a scroll of tags and monikers. The balloon "throwie" by DERM of the TKO crew entered as an uninvited comment in the footer of *South Central Dreams*, the Slauson-rails wall mural by Oaxaca's art collective Tlacolulokos featuring a young Oaxacan woman with an L.A. tattoo snapping a selfie. Names written into sidewalks in the 1940s (Smith, Johnson, Edwards, Bill, Cindy) now joined by names written into sidewalks in the 2000s (Marco, Yessika, Lorena, Pablito). A street named Brooklyn that becomes a street named Cesar E. Chavez. Or just about any section of wall piled with names in the now sealed-up autograph book of the Belmont Tunnel, the former Red Car trolley route connecting downtown to Hollywood, one of the city's greatest cathedrals of layering ever since Shandu went up with "Risko City" in 1984.

There is no history of layering without the companion history of trying to stop it from happening. Graffiti abatement and mural whitewashing are equally L.A. traditions, and the Library's photo collection is as full of photos of art and writing on walls as it is of photos of surgical-masked volunteers rolling sheets of white paint over unwanted names. The tradition is as old as city elites ordering the erasure of *América Tropical*—David Siqueiros's 1932 mural for Italian Hall depicting U.S. imperialism in Latin America and the destruction of indigenous civilization—and as recent as the Los Angeles County Metropolitan Transportation Authority applying a fresh coat of white "freeway beautification" paint over Judith F. Baca's 1984 mural *Hitting the Wall*, a commemoration of the first women to run in the Olympics marathon.

^ Standing on buckets to tag a wall near the Belmont Tunnel, the abandoned subway yard adjacent to Westlake, 2005.

‹ John Adams Junior High students paint over graffiti as part of a school cleanup effort, 1982.

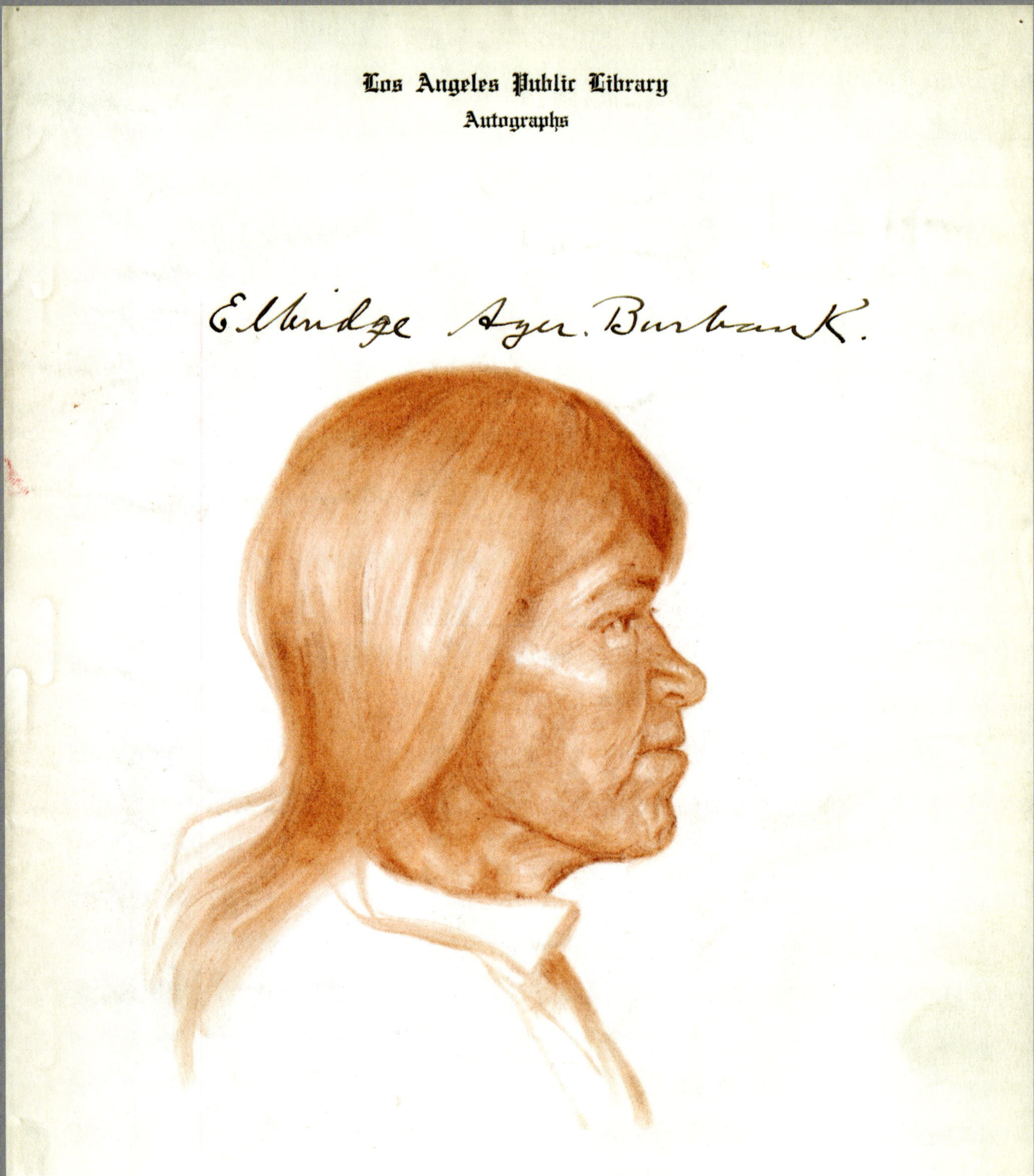

ELBRIDGE AYER BURBANK, early 1900s

In the late 1970s, the City of L.A. whitewashed the giant eyes and sneering teeth of *Caras*, the large-scale mural painted by Gronk and Willie Herrón on the City Terrace Park pavilion that had willfully become an experiment in sanctioned layering, with the artists inviting members of the Geraghty Loma gang to add their names—Tiger, Santo, Lil Rudy G, Lil Loco—atop the painting in classic Chicano wall-lettering styles. Herrón and Gronk, as members of pioneering Chicano art collective Asco, also played leading roles in one of the most famous incidents of graffiti whitewashing in the city's history: LACMA's erasure of "Spray Paint LACMA." In 1972, to protest the museum's exclusion of Chicano art from its galleries and collections, Herrón, Gronk, and Harry Gamboa—doubling down on Marcel Duchamp turning the Woolworth Building into a readymade by putting his signature on it in 1916—left their names in spray paint on one of the museum's exterior walls. "In signing the museum," scholar Chon Noriega has written, "Asco collapsed space between graffiti and conceptual art, at once fulfilling the biased thinking that justified their exclusion and refiguring the entire museum as an art object." The museum whitewashed the three signatures the day after they were written, thereby erasing what was, for twenty-four hours, the largest piece of Chicano art in existence.

Whitewashing doesn't need paint; mural-coated walls can also simply be bulldozed. When the Shell gas-station wall that housed the epic two-hundred-foot-long East Los Streetscapers mural *Filling Up on Ancient Energies* was reduced to rubble in 1988, one of the few fragments that remained amidst the toppled concrete ruins was the mural's credits section: copyright dates and hand-painted signatures of the artists that have now outlived the life of the artwork itself.

For historian William Deverell, the whitewashing and destruction of graffiti and murals has a broader corollary in the racial cover-ups of Los Angeles, the whitewashing of Mexican, Asian, African American, and indigenous histories from the city's public face, making their erasure all the more easy, strategic, and effective. Los Angeles has evolved—and continues to evolve—he writes, by "whitewashing an adobe past, even an adobe present, and adobe future," and by extension a Black past, an Asian past, and a Native American past (Carey McWilliams famously claimed L.A. kept an "Indian in the closet"), forging a visual distance and separation from the communities and histories that threaten to smudge up the clean white palettes of urban development, neighborhood revitalization, and gentrification. Similarly, Norman Klein has written of Los Angeles as a city built on erasures, removals, and evacuations—the vanishing of Chávez Ravine, the uprooting of Sonoratown and the original Chinatown—a city with a built landscape overflowing with structural and physical ghosts, palpable after-images of what once was. Just as a final piece of classic cartoon animation was the product of multiple erased versions and pencil tests, in Los Angeles Klein contends, "The final version was the whitewash, or the conciliation, the ad that went public."

Los Angeles Public Library

Autographs

BARBARA CARRASCO, 2018

Indeed, much of the labor of anti-graffiti campaigns (the City erases roughly thirty million feet of tags annually through initiatives like the current Operation Clean Sweep) is fueled by perfecting the City's ad deck. They work to insure those original pencil tests don't show through, by targeting wall writing by African American and Chicano gangs that sully neighborhoods ripe for the third-wave coffee shops and vegan bakeries of urban renewal.

The glyphs and calligraphy of gangs have been particularly influential on the stylistic and aesthetic evolution of L.A. graffiti culture. First appearing in the 1940s and gaining symbolic momentum after the anti-pachuco race war of the Zoot Suit Riots, Chicano "barrio calligraphy" has long been a powerful vehicle of messaging for Mexican American youth struggling for recognition and survival. Block lettering and point lettering, blackletter and Old English typography, all became standard tools of Chicano *placas*, or plaques. Gang writing to claim turf, beam neighborhood pride, list membership, and mourn fallen friends and family, was conceived of not as defacement, but as plaques rendered in script, grassroots text versions of a steel shield or an engraved gold-plated mount.

The frequent choice of Old English lettering was also no coincidence. Used in diplomas, degrees, death and birth certificates, and the headline logo of the *Los Angeles Times*, Old English was a plaque font, a font of authority and power that formally conveyed prestige in a public setting. It became a font of struggle and part of the visual lexicon of the Chicano civil rights movement—lettering that, like the historic murals of artists like Barbara Carrasco and Yreina D. Cervántez, demanded, out loud, on the walls, to be taken seriously and to be seen.

John F. Kennedy, then the Democratic presidential nominee, signs autographs while attending a breakfast at the Ambassador Hotel in 1960. His brother, Robert F. Kennedy, would be assassinated at the same hotel eight years later while campaigning for the Democratic presidential nomination.

FINGERS ON SAND

BUT WHAT IF THE AGE OF THE SIGNATURE IS OVER? In 2018, all major U.S. credit-card companies announced that they will no longer require signatures to process and verify customer transactions. "The signature has really outrun its useful life," a Mastercard executive recently declared. You don't need a signature to buy back-to-school outfits, toilet paper, or cases of LaCroix at Target or Walmart, and you can pay at your table without lifting a pen at Applebee's, Olive Garden, and airport gastropubs. We rarely sign checks and grumble about those in front of us in line who do, we shop online without clicking a pen (which may help us shop even more online), we sign in to devices with our faces or fingerprints, we are processed at security checkpoints with digital chips and retina scans, emails have largely replaced handwritten letters and cards sent by post, and while tags still appear on walls, the most commonly used tags are the ones we leave digitally on our social-media posts and Instagram photos. We sign more petitions than ever before—expressing outrage, demanding change, protesting inequity and discrimination—but rarely in our own hand. When we use DocuSign to validate mortgages, leases, and other official forms, the signature we leave can be one that has been digitally provided for us, one that may look nothing like the lines and curves our hand has been producing—uniquely, with all the script variations that come with the contingencies of time, place, mood, age, and bumpy flights—since we learned to write. Increasingly, a data-produced digital signature isn't even needed; data-produced digital initials will do just fine.

Even that holiest of official U.S. signatures, the presidential signature that turns bills into laws, has gone digital. In 2011, Barack Obama became the first U.S. president to use a digital signature to sign a bill into law. The device he used, the autopen—designed to sign thousands of documents quickly and hands-free with a robotic arm that creates a perfect mass-produced digital copy of an individual hand-drawn signature—has been around in various iterations since the 1950s (Truman used a version of it first) and was based on the polygraph, an analog signing machine used by Thomas Jefferson to keep replicas of his personal letters and documents. But with Obama, the autopen joined the inkwell and gold-tipped fountain pen as a standard desktop accessory.

All of this autograph digitization has, understandably, set off alarm bells. Will we ever be asked to sign our names again? Will we forget how to do it? Is this the final act in our transformation into bytes and binary code, the final curtain on our organic, analog selves? Losing our signatures is like losing our voices: Who are we as unique individuals without our unique signatures (and all of the morphing personalities, peculiar grip techniques, and aging bodies that make them what they are?) Who am I if not the bulbous off-balance swoop of my J, the wavy, tremulous line that o, s, h, k, u, n have all learned to become? Like the AI software that replicates our spoken voices after we die, the digital displacement of the autograph produces a human crisis of identity and authenticity. Without our signatures, maybe we aren't who we say are. Maybe we never were.

^ A street mural remembers singer Selena. The memorial is a painted version of the album cover for *Mi Amor Prohibido*. > Led by the Black Student Alliance, students at Los Angeles City College strike in protest of institutional racism, 1969. >> Activist Matt Redman sits with a portion of the AIDS Memorial Quilt, which commemorates those who have died of AIDS-related causes, 1988.

CITY
CAUTION

DAVID
MAYNARD
LARRY
ROCK
HUDSON

HAM ON RYE

A NOVEL BY

CHARLES BUKOWSKI

BLACK SPARROW PRESS SANTA BARBARA 1982

CHARLES BUKOWSKI, **ca. 1982 •** ***Ham on Rye***

This was part of the point Polish artist Agnieszka Kurant tried to make in 2015 with her installation *The End of Signature*. Kurant asked Guggenheim Museum visitors to feed their hand-drawn signatures into an autopen to create a digital copy. Kurant then used a software program to turn the collected signatures into one single digitally manipulated communal autograph, which was then projected as an LED neon sign onto the wall of the museum. In interviews and gallery texts, she claimed the goal was not necessarily to mourn the death of the signature by keystrokes, clicks, and code, but to suggest that maybe our faith in the signature has been misplaced all along. Our individual signatures have always been used to reinforce the myth of the atomized individual, the singular genius, the one-and-only creator. The autograph masks our connections to the larger networks and communities that make us possible, the many names behind our own that go into any single act of authorship, the villages that raise us and keep us alive and creating. The rise of crowdsourced authorship platforms like Wikipedia and collective, anonymous digital labor platforms like AmazonTurk, Kurant has suggested, may be signaling an intelligence horizon in which the one becomes the many: we all may be adding up to an anonymous single line. The autograph will be signed by all of us, all the time, at once.

Yet faith in the signature persists. We still wait in long lines to have our favorite athletes sign a basketball or a jersey, to have authors sign our copies of their books. We shake their hands, trade questions, and ask for personalized dedications. I asked Patti Smith and Valeria Luiselli to sign dedications to my daughter in books that will sit on shelves until she's old enough to read them and see that their words are especially meant for her. Artists still spend hours signing lithographs. There's a garish collector's market that still endows value upon the signature, but there is also a living-room admirer's desire for proximity and intimacy, for the knowledge that even a copy of the original contains an original signature left by an actual hand connected to the actual person who leaned over that actual canvas for weeks or years. For all of our celebrity selfies, we still want LPs, posters, napkins, and body parts signed, and the signed-memorabilia trade (certificates of authenticity included) is still holding on. And last year, in Tijuana, the signature made a stunning bid for relevance. Thousands of Central American migrants asking for asylum from the U.S. government organized themselves into a waiting list by signing what became known as "the notebook." They didn't sign with their phones or their faces or their eyes. They picked up a pen and left their name in ink on paper in the hopes—mostly in vain—that their name would be called next, that their signature would lead, at last, to sanctuary.

A man shows his tattoo at the top of the Bunker Hill Steps. It reads "Janet — Mi Amor Por Vida."

In her ongoing installation, *Crenshaw District Hieroglyphics Project*, South Central-raised artist Lauren Halsey creates a large-scale drywall pantheon of neighborhood memory. She has called it a "representational monument of community records that folks in the neighborhood will recognize as theirs." Etched in stacked gypsum panels are urban hieroglyphics of Black Los Angeles: store signage, portraits of community leaders, graffiti tags, palm trees, braids, lowriders, written messages ("We will save our people," "Be who ye is Because if you ain't who you is, You ain't who you think you is"), and scratched in her own hand, a memorial roll call of the names of black men and women killed by police. While inspired by the permanence of ancient Egyptian hieroglyphics carved in stone, Halsey carved her glyphs into the more ephemeral surfaces of drywall to highlight the precarity of her community in the face of violence, death, and gentrification—erasure and disappearance as ways of life. "I want to build the architecture from our hands to empower us and hold our narratives," she has said, "as we are being deleted and shuffled around."

As this book went to press, rapper, entrepreneur, and community activist Nipsey Hussle became one of the deleted, shot down in front of his clothing store in South Los Angeles. In the days and weeks since, Angelenos of all stripes have visited the site—just as so many did after the deaths of Selena, Elliott Smith, Chalino Sanchez, Prince, and Juan Gabriel—to leave their names and their messages on walls and sidewalks, using all of the familiar tools of the graffiti, mural, and tagging trades. The tradition of the autograph and the tradition of the tag and the throw-up have trained us well. When we want to remember, when we want to hold off forgetting, when we want to make visible, when we want to build monuments to our presence, when we want to "hold our narratives," we reach for something to write with and something to write on.

We stitch the dead into quilts. We ink their lives into our skin. We give loss a name. We leave our marks.

Even in the midst of our digital moment, thousands of people, tourists and residents alike, flock to local beaches to leave perhaps the most iconic and evergreen L.A. autograph of all. They use their fingers to drag their names and initials in the sand, digging curving canals that spell out "I Love You" or "Will you marry me?" They do this knowing full well that the tide will soon rise, that water will wash it away, if the wind or a destructive little brother doesn't get there first. They sign the sand not out of arrogance but out of humility. They leave their names in the sand because they know that neither they nor their names will last forever.

Massachusetts Senator Ted Kennedy signs autographs while visiting John F. Kennedy Elementary School in Compton, 1971.

Dwight D. Eisenhower signs autographs on his way to Palm Desert after finishing his final term as president. The *Herald Examiner* reported that he agreed to give "just one" autograph, then continued signing for a half hour, 1961.

CHARLINE, late 1800s

DISPATCHES FROM THE CITY BENEATH

SUSAN A. PHILLIPS

CHARLINE

Somebody didn't like her. She wrote her name with a nail, boring it into the soft plaster of the wall to decorate her letters' ends with dots. She wrote her last name too, but the letters HA are all that remain of it. *Charline* appears on a wall covered with numerous names, initials, and signatures, most of which date from the late nineteenth century. It's the oldest graffiti in the city. One thing I've learned in my years of graffiti research is this simple equation: old infrastructure equals old writing. If you want to find the old stuff, you have to go to the old places, whether they are buildings, bridges, storm-drain tunnels, or city blocks. The 1862 Civil War–era powder magazine where Charline's name appears is one of the oldest structures in Los Angeles. The names that continue to adorn it boast dates ranging from 1873 to 1902, with some contemporary pieces thrown in. Other girls are here as well: Rhoda and Nellie etched their names into bricks alongside numerous soldiers, boys, and men. Eventually, the powder magazine became a meat locker and was encased by another building. When that building was demolished in the early 1980s, the rediscovered powder magazine was designated as a historic monument in order to save it from the wrecking ball. An LAPL photograph of it shows cows and sheep with two children resting against its walls. Wilmington's bucolic aspect in those days might come as a surprise to some. Charline's is one of the larger inscriptions on the building. Later, someone crossed it out with an X.

Like I said, somebody didn't like Charline.

In the history of L.A. graffiti, girls are everywhere, but they're playing a boy's game. Aside from Charline's cross-out (Nellie could have been the culprit, after all), how many times have I seen women's names defamed, defaced, and defiled for the amusement of men? The thing about Charline, though, is that she might have been a *Charlie*—a *Charlie* with weird spacing and the suggestion of an N in the old plaster, rather than the N itself. With graffiti, you never know for sure.

WILLIE G.

Willie G. was probably a worker. He was a bartender, doorman, bouncer, washroom attendant, or stockroom assistant who worked at a saloon in the King Edward Hotel. There have always been bars at the King Eddy—either aboveground ones in the days before and after prohibition, or the infamous underground one in the basement during the speakeasy years between 1918 and 1933. Prohibition came early to L.A. Either way, Willie G. spent a lot of time at the King Edward Hotel. His pencil letters are thumbnail small, some smaller. His work is, in fact, the tiniest graffiti I have ever seen. Diminutive hearts, circles, or squares intertwine with the teensiest of initials: *WG*. Willie wrote his initials over thirty times in what used to be the basement bathroom—not on the walls where patrons wrote near the stall, urinals, and sink. That area is covered with pricks, blowjob fantasies, and homoerotic invitations to go 50–50. Only one has a date: 1922. I sometimes imagine that Willie might have been responsible for the feats of graffiti removal in that bathroom, attempts to rub out copious penciled profanities, or the painting of certain walls a dark gray to cancel out the color of graphite markings.

Graffiti abatement was already a thing in the 1920s.

Willie G. sometimes carved his initials, giving the letters a more contemporary, angular quality. At a certain point, he wrote his full name: Willie Garing. I found a number of Willie or William Garings in the U.S. census. Two were African American men from Louisiana and Mississippi—they seemed too young, with birthdates in 1913 and 1918. Another Willie Garing was a man of German descent who worked as a bartender in a saloon in Chicago at the time of the 1910 census. The Chicago location doesn't preclude him from being in Los Angeles in the teens or twenties. On the contrary, Chicago was a hub for train travel or hobo-style freight hopping. Willie could have caught a westbound to L.A. and brought his bartending skills to the King Eddy. The whole speakeasy has a faux *biergarten* flavor, covered as it is with mural depictions of wooden beer barrels and Hansel-and-Gretel houses. Rumor has it that the paintings of trees on the basement's main walls somehow provide maps to other speakeasy locations in downtown, with their crooked branches pointing the way. I don't believe it. What I do know is simpler: I know Willie G. He was there, and he left a mark.

WILLIE GARING "WILLIE G.", 1920s

W.G
WG

A-NO. 1, circa 1914

A-NO. 1

While Willie G. may have been a master of the miniscule, hobo A-No. 1, a decade earlier, was more like the king of the colossal. Scaling letter sizes up or down is a special skill all graffiti writers share. Lord Byron excelled at it, carving his name all over the ruins of Europe so that it could be seen from afar. Writers understand the marriage of name and space in extraordinary ways. Today's graffiti writers frequently do their work in the dark, their letters are often larger than themselves, and they stand cheek to cheek with the wall in order to produce them.

Graffiti is a complex craft. If you don't believe me, get a spray can and try to do something with it. That goes for any of the common graffiti media: streaker (paint stick), roller, white-out bottle, or even a knife for carving. Odds are, whatever you produce will look terrible. Graffiti writers know their media intimately, practice what they do, hone their skill, and understand the relationship between their craft, the scale of letters, and the built environment. They see their own names through the eyes of others and through the vantage of places where they are not.

A-No. 1 was a man dedicated to his craft. He carved his name all over the United States, wrote a dozen books in which hobo graffiti was featured, and, as if that weren't enough, promoted his story in every town he visited by stopping in at the local rag. He was jailed for graffiti eighty years before the notorious L.A. writer Chaka would be, in the 1990s. Both served five-month sentences. People sometimes find surviving A-No. 1 carvings in the United States. Two possible instances of his name are here in Los Angeles, one dated 1914. They're nothing too special, they're of smallish stature, and it's hard to know if they're his for sure. Dial it back a few years, though, to San Francisco. In A-No. 1's Bay Area hometown, he used a pickaxe to carve his name on Yerba Buena Island, rendering the letters so large that they could be seen from passing ships. His work attracted the attention of a maritime commuter associated with the upcoming 1909 Portola Festival, and a light bulb went off in the man's head: *Why should not the words "Portola Festival" greet the eyes of passers-by to promote the festival, rather than the name of this confounded hobo?* It took a month to construct an official sign with forty-five-foot high letters measuring thirteen hundred feet long. The so-called "monster sign" generated global interest: it was said to be the largest of its kind in the world. A photograph of the "Portola Festival" sign survives, but A-No. 1's original carving is predictably lost to history.

And the concept of the outsize billboard was born on the back of a graffiti writer.

ANONYMOUS SEAFARER, 1962 · Window, Overlooking, Ocean waves, Well.

ANONYMOUS SEAFARER

There's something beautiful about the time before the spray can, when the media for writing graffiti came directly from the city itself: wet concrete, railroad tar, rocks on the ground, spikes, nails, burned wood. Kids would wander then, pick up a stone, and write on the walls, just like that. Serendipity.

For working people, sometimes their occupation places media in hand—chalk, grease pencil, shoeshine, paint. If labor grants the means, it also offers the opportunity: isolated places for production, from rail yards to the soundstages of Hollywood. But medium and space are not enough. One additional ingredient provides motive, and that is boredom. Sheer, unadulterated boredom. Boredom that emerges from the drudgery of blue-collar labor. There's more to it than that, but across multiple examples and contexts, that labor-based trifecta of materials, space, and idle time tends to spark graffiti's genesis.

Graffiti at the Ports of Los Angeles and Long Beach comes in lengthy horizontals, written on the dock face with the paint that seafarers once used to touch up their behemoth vessels. The sailors would have just come into port after weeks or months at sea. All they wanted was to get to shore, but they were stuck scraping rust and repainting the hull. On little skiffs with paint in hand, seafarers from Russia to Israel would write out ship names, personal names, place-names, and dates in Thai, Greek, Hebrew, Tamil, and Chinese, to name a few. This is true alphabet soup—a crash course in global geography, in the world's scripts, and in its calendrical systems. Most of what I know about the world's languages comes from the harbor. The place is a most patient professor. Its tactile, sensory pedagogy combines with oil and salt, exhaust and fish. Lessons shift with ebb or flood tides. The messages are simple: a ship name, a date, sometimes the callout of a hometown or a specific sailor's name. This particular genre of graffiti might be a thing of the past—seafarers can't use paint in the harbor any longer. Despite that ban, there's a whole history there for the taking, in the words of generations of container-ship sailors.

In 1962, an anonymous seafarer wrote below the dock face in the oldest part of the harbor. His Chinese characters are visible only at low tide. The rest of the time, the piece remains submerged. It's been partially destroyed—less from wearing seawater than from a concrete intervention involving a drainage pipe. In the fifty-plus years since the composition was written, over forty thousand tides have moved the piece between visibility and invisibility: *Window, Overlooking, Ocean waves, Well.* The seafarer's words present a view from inside, the window of a ship looking out onto miles of ocean.

Through graffiti, people tie themselves to social and physical landscapes. The writing of women, children, sailors, workers, hobos, gang members, and union members weaves those ties into the fabric of the city in multiple formats and for multiple reasons. Graffiti's sitedness, its condensed or distilled nature, and its indexicality—its ability to act like a fingerprint—make it a mode of expression stripped down to its barest elements, contained in keywords, names, and dates. No matter how elaborately adorned, the most common of graffiti's stripped-down elements is the name—the tag, the moniker, the *placa*, the signature.

HOBBIE

If mortality defines the human condition, the signature outlasts it. Though it may not always be a signature, graffiti is always an auto-graph, if we take that word in its literal sense, as in a writing of one's self.

Signatures have legal value because of their direct connection to the person. They have value at the bank, when taking out a loan or signing checks. They also have value on the streets, where being "up" brings respect in the eyes of graffiti insiders, and where police tally cumulative graffiti acts to be used against writers in courts of law.

A signature is a representation of ourselves, a material trace that connects our internal state to something external, like an existential echo.

I brought Christine Shedley to see her grandfather's name in chalk and charcoal on the Holly Street Bridge in Pasadena: *Hobart Gormley*, written circa 1926. I had tracked Christine down through Hobart's obituary and her Facebook page. We met and talked, and we eventually went to the bridge. Hobart had taken custody of Christine at a critical time in her life, and she was overcome when she saw his *Hobbie*.

"Oh my goodness," she said. "Papa." She said her heart was happy to be able to see his writing, that it helped her to believe the other things he told her about his life. Of the graffiti, she said, "I never imagined that it would still be here. It's amazing for it to stand. It's ninety years? It's almost a century, and to still be here. That's amazing. It speaks volumes to me about him. Because that's how strong HE is."

Since our first visit, the bridge has become where Christine goes to see her grandfather. She says she wants to visit him where he was alive, rather than to visit him where he's buried. She sometimes comes alone, or she brings her children. She reflected: "It just makes me think. It's never really over. Now my son can bring his sons to see what his great grampa did. The story never ends."

A project on signatures, or autographs, through the optic of graffiti creates multiple centers that decentralize, level, and flip the archive. Graffiti reverses the telling of history by putting it into the hands of everyday people. They don't write history intentionally. Rather they participate in the making of the city by writing their names. L.A. has had many maniacal writers through time, and it still does. I know some of them. Their foibles aren't so different from the weaknesses, compulsions, and anxieties we all share. They're just visible in a different way.

Graffiti makes the city a giant, self-published essay. It's my favorite kind of puzzle, with pieces scattered all over neighborhoods, under bridges, and in waterways. In a city as segregated as Los Angeles, the statement *I was here* is a radical act. That act—the act of the signature—is a story that adds to the city's history and is the stamp of its people.

HOBART GORMLEY, "HOBBIE," 1926

Hobbie

Kenny Washington, who played football for the Hollywood Bears and the Los Angeles Rams, signs an autograph for a beauty queen, circa 1960.

A teenager from the San Fernando Valley wears a "Collector Shirt" made by designer Phil Rose. Featuring the signatures of movie stars on the front, it came with its own permanent fabric marker so friends could add their autographs to the back, 1962.

An officer deciphers gang graffiti with the help of two young men in East Los Angeles' Happy Valley, 1965.

RIVERBED ROLL CALLS

CHAZ BOJÓRQUEZ

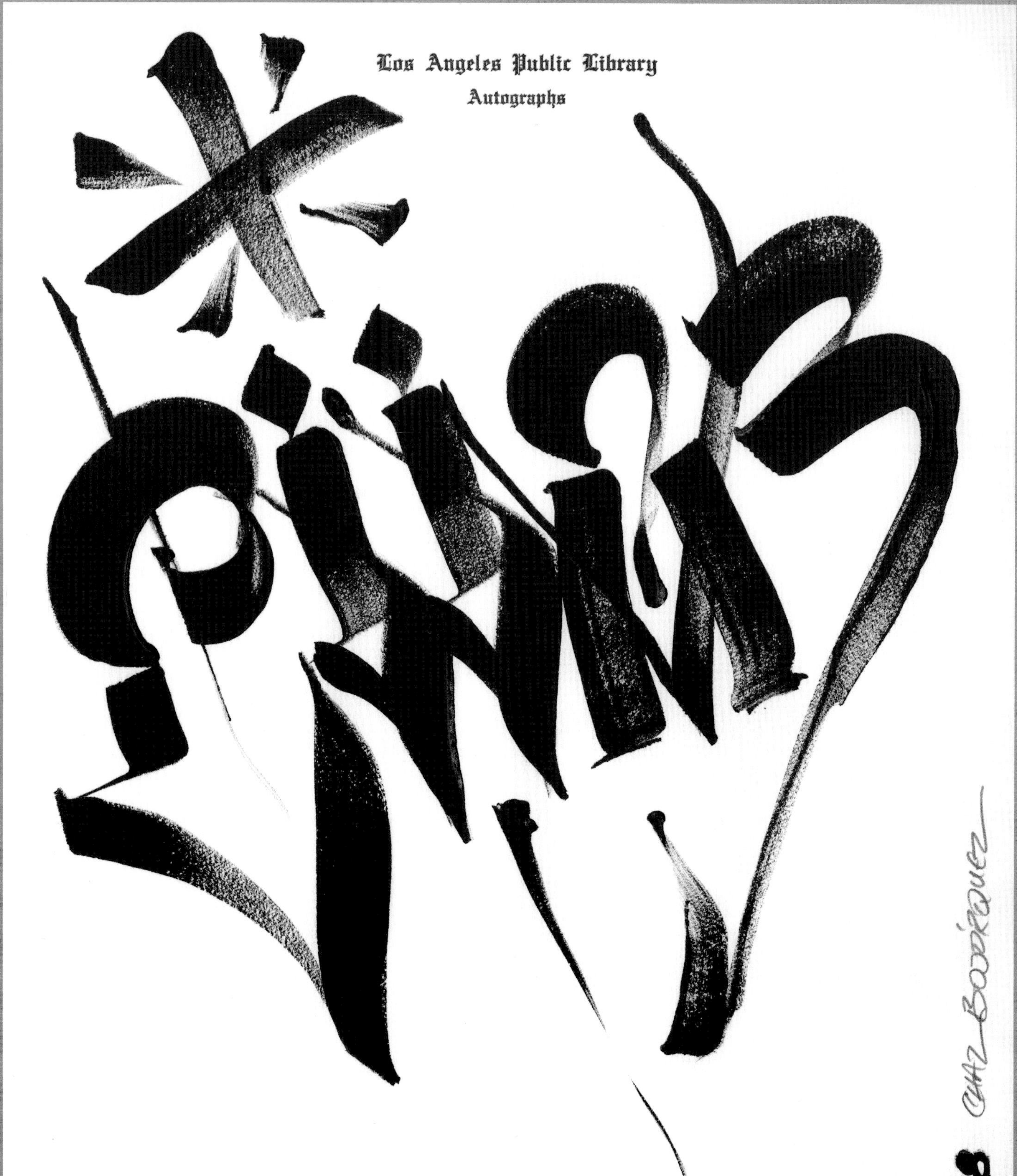

CHAZ BOJÓRQUEZ, 2018

I GREW UP IN HIGHLAND PARK, but if you had asked me, "What's your homeland? What's your influence? Where do you get your spirit from?" the answer wasn't East L.A. It was Hollywood, because of all the rock and roll I experienced when I was young. I wouldn't cruise Whittier Boulevard or the streets of Montebello, like my cousins. I was a rock-and-roller first, and I loved Grauman's Chinese Theatre. When I would see the handprints and footprints of all the famous actors, I would stick my footprints inside theirs; I would put my hands in their handprints. When I would see the sidewalks, I could almost fit my finger into the lines of their writing and mimic and reproduce their actual signature as they were leaving it in the concrete. It made me feel like it was mine, like I was a celebrity too.

I had the same feeling when I started writing and painting on walls. It makes you known, makes you immortal, makes you think you can last forever. It empowers you.

My mom grew up downtown and went to Belmont High School, but she liked to hang out in Hollywood. She went to all the 1940s movie premieres and kept an autograph book. She was really fascinated by movies and movie stars, and I grew up fascinated by the mysteries of the people behind those signatures, just as I would be fascinated by the mysteries of the people behind all the graffiti I saw in the neighborhood. Later I would end up working a stint in Hollywood. Me and a friend who had just been released from a military prison got jobs doing paint stuff for productions in Hollywood and in these boutique movie studios—we did movie posters, movie titles, and all that, and became junior art directors. But I told myself, "If I'm ever going to be that painter, that artist that I've always wanted to be, I need to quit this job. You have to jump all in. No safety net. You have to be all in to be a painter."

My journey as a painter began much earlier, when as a kid I started going down to the Arroyo Seco riverbed with my friends. But they all gave up, so I ended up going alone. I would take two six-packs—one full of beer and one full of spray cans—and my boom box. The river was full of broken bottles, and at night the moonlight made it look like a diamond-studded highway. It sparkled at night, and with the freeway next to it, the headlights of the speeding cars would flicker on and off on the concrete walls. It reminded me of a black-and-white Hollywood movie with the picture flashing on and off. It had a real noir feeling to it. I felt very comfortable down there all by myself. Gang members would see me and just think I was crazy. I kept going down there for at least ten years. It was my canvas, miles and miles of my own personal canvas.

The riverbed was mostly vertical, but it would also tilt and had a 45-degree slant to it. You could walk on it. You could be painting and walking on the surface at the same time. You could make letters as tall as you wanted and as long as you wanted, as long as the paint lasted.

Los Angeles Public Library

Autographs

PRISCILLA FERNANDEZ

1981 – ?

THINGS THAT REMIND ME OF HIGHLAND PARK

1. KARATE @ THE REC. CENTER ... SENSEI: Shannon Clear?
2. HIGHLAND THEATRE
3. BASEBALL GAMES
4. JUMPING OVER THE FENCE, SWIMMING IN THE REC CENTER POOL
5. ST. IGNATIUS
6. THRIFTY 35¢ ICE CREAM SCOOPS W/ MY DAD
7. ELOTES, SHAVED ICE, CHICHARRONES
8. WEINERSNITCHEL HOTDOGS – HOPEFULLY THEY COME UP W/ A VEGGIE DOG
9. I ♥ HIGHLAND PARK
10. CAN'T FORGET ABOUT THE AVENUES & HLP

... Highland PaRK (HLP) looks really different now ... lucky for me ... I ~~[illegible]~~ fell in love with HLP before it became "Highland Park"

PRISCILLA FERNANDEZ, 2018

The riverbed wasn't blank—there was already a lot of graffiti down there. The first graffiti I ever saw was there in the river's drainage holes. They were maybe about four feet high. As long as you stooped over, you could walk back in there for a couple of miles. There was graffiti from the 1930s and '40s that young people had written with the smoke of their candles and Zippo lighters loaded with kerosene that could make puffy little linings. I never felt scared down there because there was always graffiti around me. I felt like it was protecting me.

When I started doing my first graffiti tags in 1969, I couldn't afford a spray can. I used a water bottle, and I stole some ink, and I mixed it with water. I went out and just sprayed it, like doing your laundry, spraying on a shirt. Tshh, tshh, tshh. I eventually bought a spray can and also saved up for a stencil. I'd seen stencils in Mexico, because the political parties used them all over Tijuana in big one- or two-color wall designs. I bought myself a large sheet of Mylar, which was the most expensive, the most cutting-edge plastic at that time, and I made my drawing, the skull that became my signature image, "Señor Suerte."

I wasn't trying to be an anarchist. I wasn't angry. I didn't have any vendetta for the government or the city or anything like that. I felt that what I was doing was an improvement on the city. I wasn't trying to impose myself on the public. I already felt that I had something important to say, and I wasn't alone. I had this whole history of graffiti behind me, of Highland Park, The Avenues, Dogtown, White Fence, CP boys. I felt that I was part of that community. I didn't feel like I was being an individual, arrogant artist who's trying to find his own personal fame. I felt like part of a group, of a movement. I knew from the very beginning that what I was doing was art, and it was noble. It was the real thing. I was not doing trash art or gutter art or however else curators and art critics were describing graffiti. To me, this was fine art.

I went to Chouinard Art Institute and did figure drawing at the same time that I started doing tagging and creating my stencil in the streets. I did my graffiti for ten years and did art school for ten years, but I kept them separate. But soon they merged—after traveling around the world, I realized completely that language and culture are fine art. In 1980, I did my first painting, *Placa/Rollcall*. I started thinking, "How can I make my relations as strong as a gang? How can I define myself by having my own gang behind me?" The roll call is a list of who is in your gang, which could mean fellow gang members in the tradition, or it could be your co-workers, or it could be your family. Basically, it's your telephone book—all your influences, all your relations, all your history, all your loves. In the painting, which is now in the Smithsonian, there are partial names on the top, bottom, and sides because the list is bigger than the layout of the painting. It's bigger than the canvas.

We are always going to want to leave roll calls, to tag names, to give and collect autographs, no matter where—in a book, in a gallery, in wet concrete, on the walls of the riverbed. I believe we all want our presence to be reckoned with. Everybody has a little wish to be recognized, to be famous, to be remembered for something important. That drive will never diminish. It will always be part of us.

Why do I draw? Why do I paint? Because I've got something to say.

An artist holds up a painting in front of Belmont Tunnel near Westlake. Originally designed for the Pacific Electric Railway, the tunnel was abandoned in 1955. In the ensuing decades it became an iconic location for graffiti artists, 1994.

A survivor of the Armenian genocide shows tattoos created by the family that rescued her, 1929.

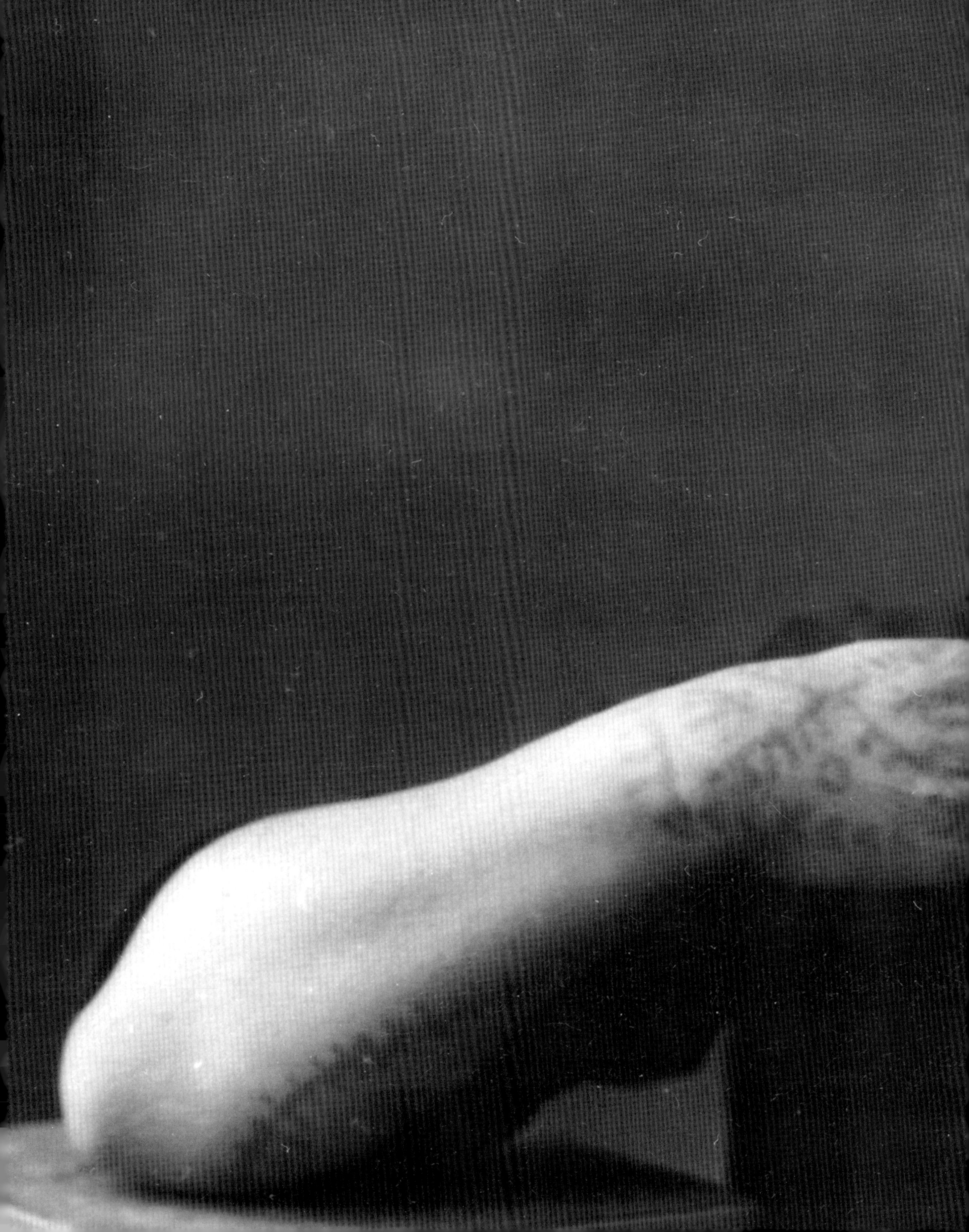

IMPROVEMENTS ON THE PAGE OF THE CITY: A GALLERY

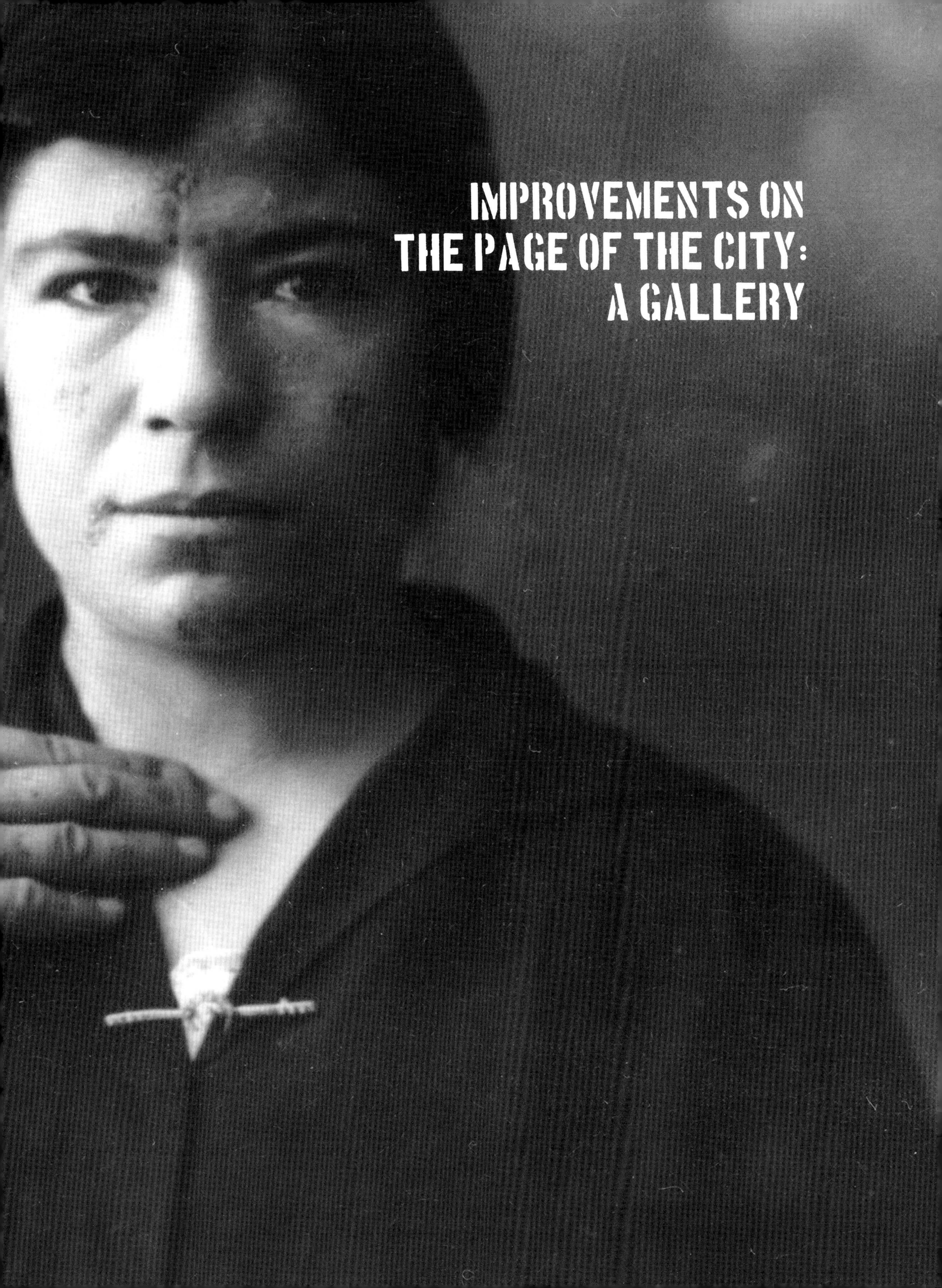

Los Angeles Public Library

Autographs

Photo. © copyright 1900 by Chas. F. Lummis.

Going to the mountains
is going home

John Muir

JOHN MUIR, early 1900s • Going to the mountains is going home. The page includes a cyanotype by Charles Lummis.

Los Angeles Public Library

Autographs

Life is Good. Good and going!
You can help – or you can hinder,
Give new fire – or be a cinder –
That's worth knowing.

Charlotte Perkins Gilman.
New York June 1st – 1910

CHARLOTTE PERKINS GILMAN, 1910 • Life is Good. Good and going! / You can help — or you can hinder, / Give new fire — or be a cinder — / That's worth knowing.

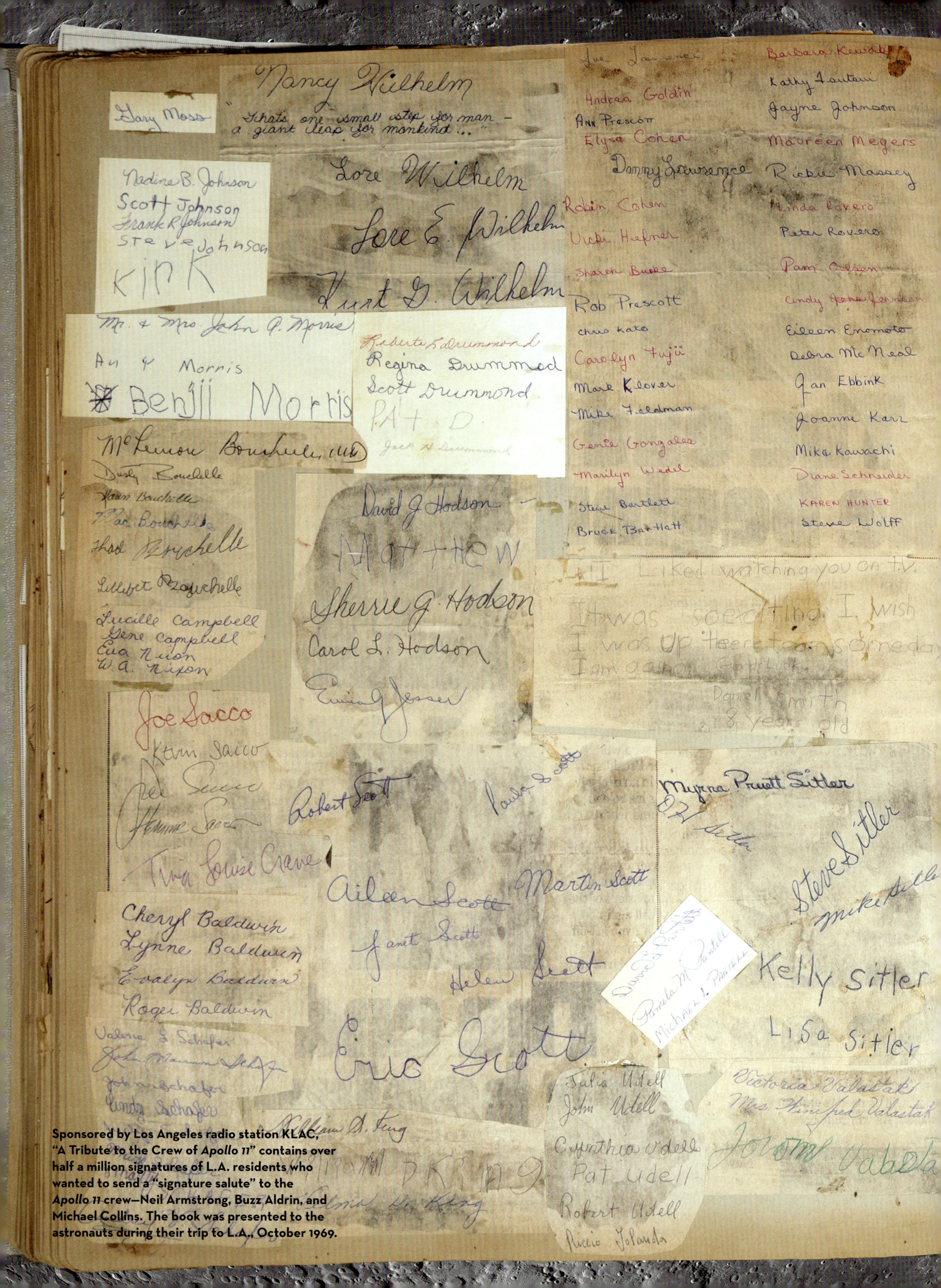

Sponsored by Los Angeles radio station KLAC, "A Tribute to the Crew of *Apollo 11*" contains over half a million signatures of L.A. residents who wanted to send a "signature salute" to the *Apollo 11* crew—Neil Armstrong, Buzz Aldrin, and Michael Collins. The book was presented to the astronauts during their trip to L.A., October 1969.

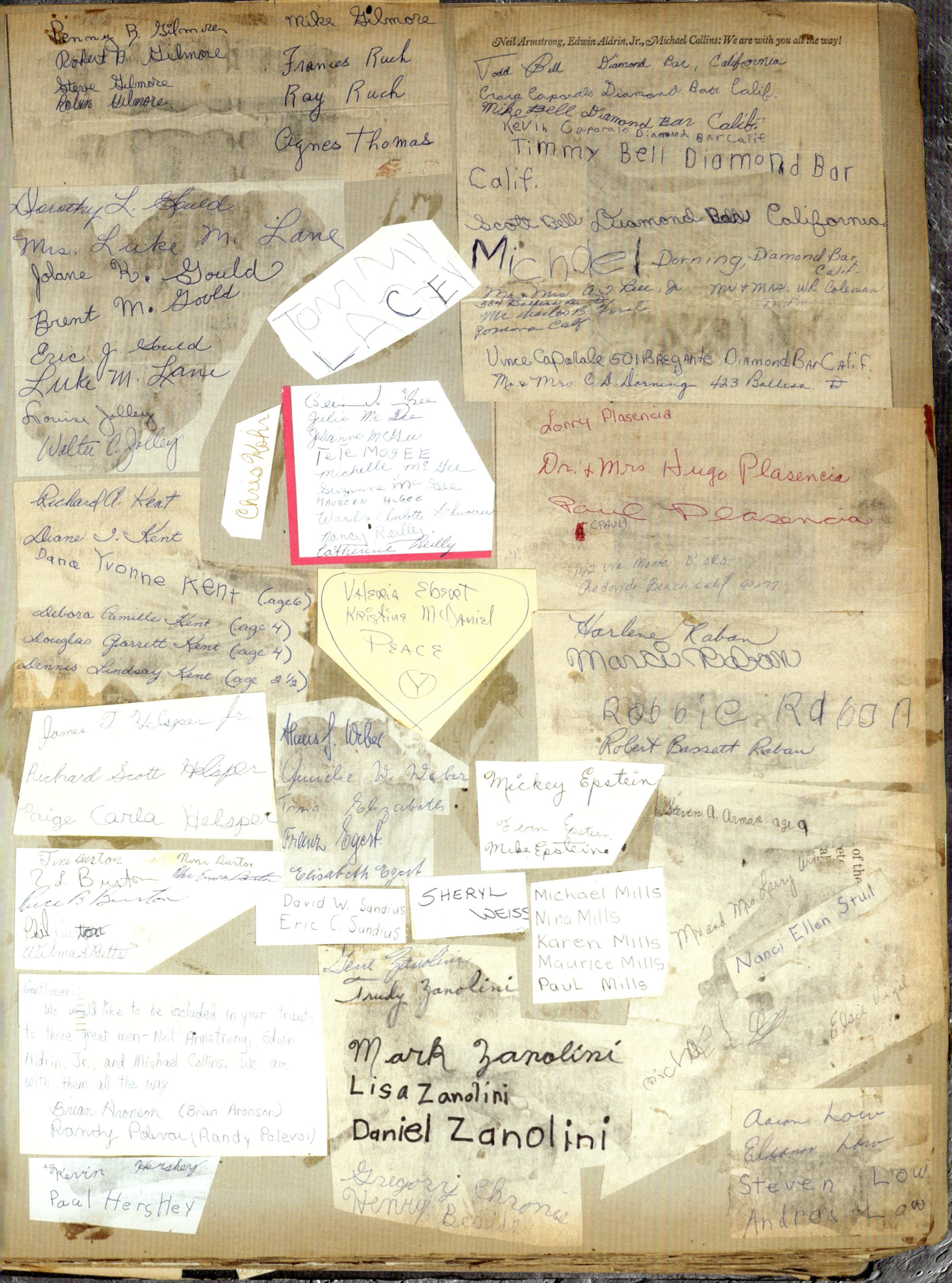

Robert B. Gilmore
Steve Gilmore
Robin Gilmore
Mike Gilmore
Frances Ruch
Ray Ruch
Agnes Thomas
Neil Armstrong, Edwin Aldrin, Jr., Michael Collins: We are with you all the way!
Todd Bell Diamond Bar, California
Mike Bell Diamond Bar Calif.
Timmy Bell Diamond Bar Calif.
Scott Bell Diamond Bar California
Michael Dorning, Diamond Bar Calif.
Vince Capolale 501 Bregante Diamond Bar Calif.
Mr & Mrs C.A. Dorning 423 Ballena D
Dorothy L. Gould
Mrs. Luke M. Lane
Jolane K. Gould
Brent M. Gould
Eric J. Gould
Luke M. Lane
Louise Jolley
Walter C. Jolley
TOMMY LACEY
Chris Kohr
Julie McGee
Tete McGee
Michelle McGee
Suzanne McGee
Maureen McGee
Nancy Reilly
Catherine Reilly
Larry Plasencia
Dr. & Mrs Hugo Plasencia
Paul Plasencia
142 Via Monte D'Oro
Redondo Beach Calif 90277
Richard A. Kent
Diane J. Kent
Dana Yvonne Kent (age 6)
Debora Camille Kent (age 4)
Douglas Garrett Kent (age 4)
Dennis Lindsay Kent (age 2½)
Valeria Ebert
Kristina McDaniel
PEACE
Harlene Raban
Marcie Raban
Robbie Raban
Robert Bassett Raban
James T. Helsper Jr.
Richard Scott Helsper
Paige Carla Helsper
Mickey Epstein
Fern Epstein
Mike Epstein
Steven A. Arman age 9
David W. Sundius
Eric C. Sundius
SHERYL WEISS
Michael Mills
Nina Mills
Karen Mills
Maurice Mills
Paul Mills
Nanci Ellen Stull
Gentlemen:
We would like to be included in your tribute to three great men - Neil Armstrong, Edwin Aldrin, Jr., and Michael Collins. We are with them all the way.
Brian Aronson (Brian Aronson)
Randy Polevoi (Randy Polevoi)
Trudy Zanolini
Mark Zanolini
Lisa Zanolini
Daniel Zanolini
Gregory Chrona
Kevin Hershey
Paul Hershey
Aaron Low
Steven Low

Los Angeles Public Library

Autographs

I've been in this town so long that back in the city I've been taken for lost
and gone and unknown for a long long time —
Fell in love years ago with an innocent girl in the Spanish & Indian Home
of the Heroes and Villains
once at night, Cotillion-squared the fight & she was right in the rain
of the bullets that eventually brought her down —
But she's still dancing in the night, unafraid of what a dude'll do
in a town full of Heroes & Villains
Stand or Fall, I know there shall be peace in the Valley
and it's all an affair of my life with the Heroes and Villains
our children were raised - you know they suddenly rise —
They started slow, long ago, head to toes healthy, wealthy,
and often wise —
I've been in this town so long
So long to the city —
I'm fit with the stuff -
To ride in the rough -
And sonny, down snuff -
I'm alright -
By the heroes & villains
Heroes & villains: Just see what you've done done
to the church of the American Indian

Van Dyke Parks
Los Angeles
2018

VAN DYKE PARKS, 2018 • I've been in this town for so long that back in the city I've been taken for lost and gone and unknown for a long long time — / Fell in love years ago with an innocent girl in the Spanish and Indian Home of the Heroes and Villains / Once at night, Cotillion-squared the fight & she was right in the rain of the bullets that eventually brought her down — / But she's still dancing in the night, unafraid of what a dude'll do in a town full of Heroes & Villains — / Stand or Fall, I know there shall be peace in the Valley / And it's all an affair of my life with the Heroes and Villains / Our children were raised – you know they suddenly rise — / They started slow, long ago, head to toe, healthy, wealthy / and often wise — / I've been in this town so long / So long to the city / I'm fit with the stuff / To ride in the rough / And sonny, down snuff — / I'm alright — / By the heroes & villains / Heroes and villains: Just see what you've done done / To the church of the American Indian

SHIZU SALDAMANDO, 2019

Los Angeles Public Library

Autographs

OH SAY CAN YOU.

HELL NAW I CAN'T SEE, BECAUSE YOU JUST CRACKED ME IN MY HEAD.
FOR STANDING UP FOR MY RIGHTS.
AND THE BLOOD THAT IS GALLANTLY STREAMING FROM THE WOUND IS BLINDING MY SIGHT.
NAW I CAN'T SEE!

MY COUNTRY TIS OF THEE SWEET LAND OF LIBERTY
LAND WHERE MY FATHER DIED, HOME WHERE MY BABIES CRIED.
WE WERE BROUGHT HERE IN CHAINS AND WE STILL ENDURE THOSE PAINS

I THOUGHT I LIVED IN THE LAND OF THE FREE AND THE HOME OF THE BRAVE
BUT SOMEHOW OR NOTHER I STILL FEEL LIKE A SLAVE.

WE FOUGHT YOUR WARS, WE CLEANED YOUR FLOORS.
SO WE CONTINUE TO KNOCK ON YOUR DOOR... THAT YOU HAVE YET TO ANSWER...

SWEET LAND OF LIBERTY WHAT HAVE YOU GIVEN TO THEE?
YEARS OF HOPE AND YOUR FOREARM AROUND MY THROAT!

AMERICA, AMERICA GOD SHED ITS GRACE ON THEE
BUT SOMEHOW OR ANOTHER YOU SEEM TO HAVE FORGOT ABOUT ME.

NAW I CAN'T SEE!

YOU REDLINE ME, OH SAY CAN YOU SEE THE DETRIMENT YOU HAVE BROUGHT ONTO THEE?
YOU CRIMINALIZE AND DEMONIZE MY LOOKS.
YOU REMOVE ME FROM YOUR BOOKS.

BUT STILL I RIZE, STILL I RIZE! TO CLAIM THE PRIZE
THAT WAS PROMISED TO ME.
BY THE POWERS THAT BE.
EQUAL RIGHTS, JOBS AND LIBERTY!

HELLMUTHERFUCKING NAW I CAN'T SEE!!!

RON FINLEY.
If you're not at the table, You're on the menu.

PLANT SOME SHIT!

RON FINLEY, 2018

Los Angeles Public Library
Autographs

I'm like the palm trees in L.A.
Twice removed from Sham
But when I was growing up nobody knew where I was from
I'd tell them that I'm Syrian
They stood there looking curious
Start speaking to me in Spanish
Some would even speak in tongues
I wasn't offended
Never am
Couldn't have an agenda
Well aware of the privileges my new blue passport rendered
Nose clean
No angel
but no fiend
No playboy
but no chump
No label could own me
If only
I'd swear more
Say I don't care more
But those who know me know That isn't me
so I'm here more
Showing up for my fam
Being present when I can
Recognizing it's a blessing to caress my Mother's hand
Or be given a Microphone to address another Man
And remind him I'm no lesser of a Man.

In Time a Rhyme will likely tell which Poet manages
To leave an indelible mark on
The City of Los Angeles.

SinSyrianly Yours,

-

OMAR OFFENDUM, 2018

Los Angeles Public Library
Autographs

O Great Spirit

Whose voice I hear in the winds, and whose breath
gives life to all the world, hear me!
I am small and weak, I need your
strength and wisdom.

Let me walk in Beauty, and make my eyes
ever behold the red and purple sunset-
Make my Hands respect the things you have
made and my ears sharp to hear your voice.

Make me wise so that I may understand the things
you have taught my people.

Let me Learn the lessons you have hidden in every
leaf and rock.

I seek strength, not to be greater than my brother,
but to fight my greatest enemy-myself.

Make me always Ready to come to you with cleand
hands and Straigt eyes.

So when life fades, as the fading sunset,
my spirit may come to you without shame.

Native American Prayer — Guadalupe Mancias
6/08/18

GUADALUPE MANCIAS, 2018

KARI BARBA, 2018, Outer Limits Tattoo

KULAPAT YANTRASAST, 2018

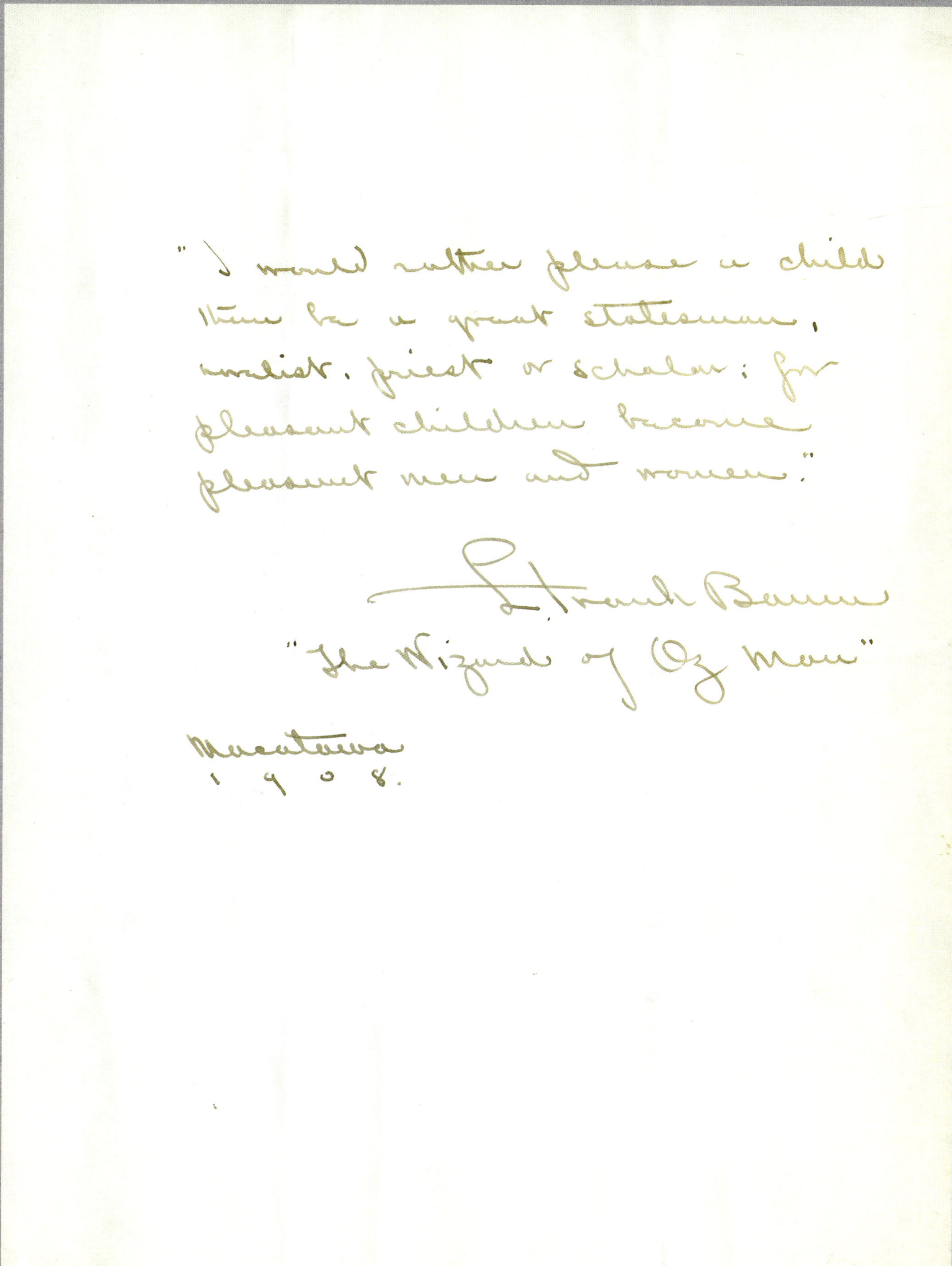

"I would rather please a child than be a great statesman, muralist, priest or scholar; for pleasant children become pleasant men and women."

L. Frank Baum

"The Wizard of Oz Man"

Macatawa
1908.

L. FRANK BAUM, "THE WIZARD OF OZ MAN," 1908 • I would rather please a child than be a great statesman, muralist, priest, or scholar; for pleasant children become pleasant men and women.

FREDERIC REMINGTON, early 1900s

PHANTOM STREET ARTIST, 2019

Los Angeles Public Library

Autographs

Good Evening. Simone. Up Grade. Shugga. Skid Row.
One Of Skid Row Finest Indepedent Artist, Writer,
Performer. Shugga. Skidrow. #1 Film Capitol Of
The World. Thank you. Shugga

SHUGGA, 2018 • Good Evening. Simone. UpGrade. Shugga. Skid Row. One of Skid Row Finest Independent Artist, Writer, Performer. Shugga. Skidrow. #1 Film Capitol Of The World. Thank you. Shugga

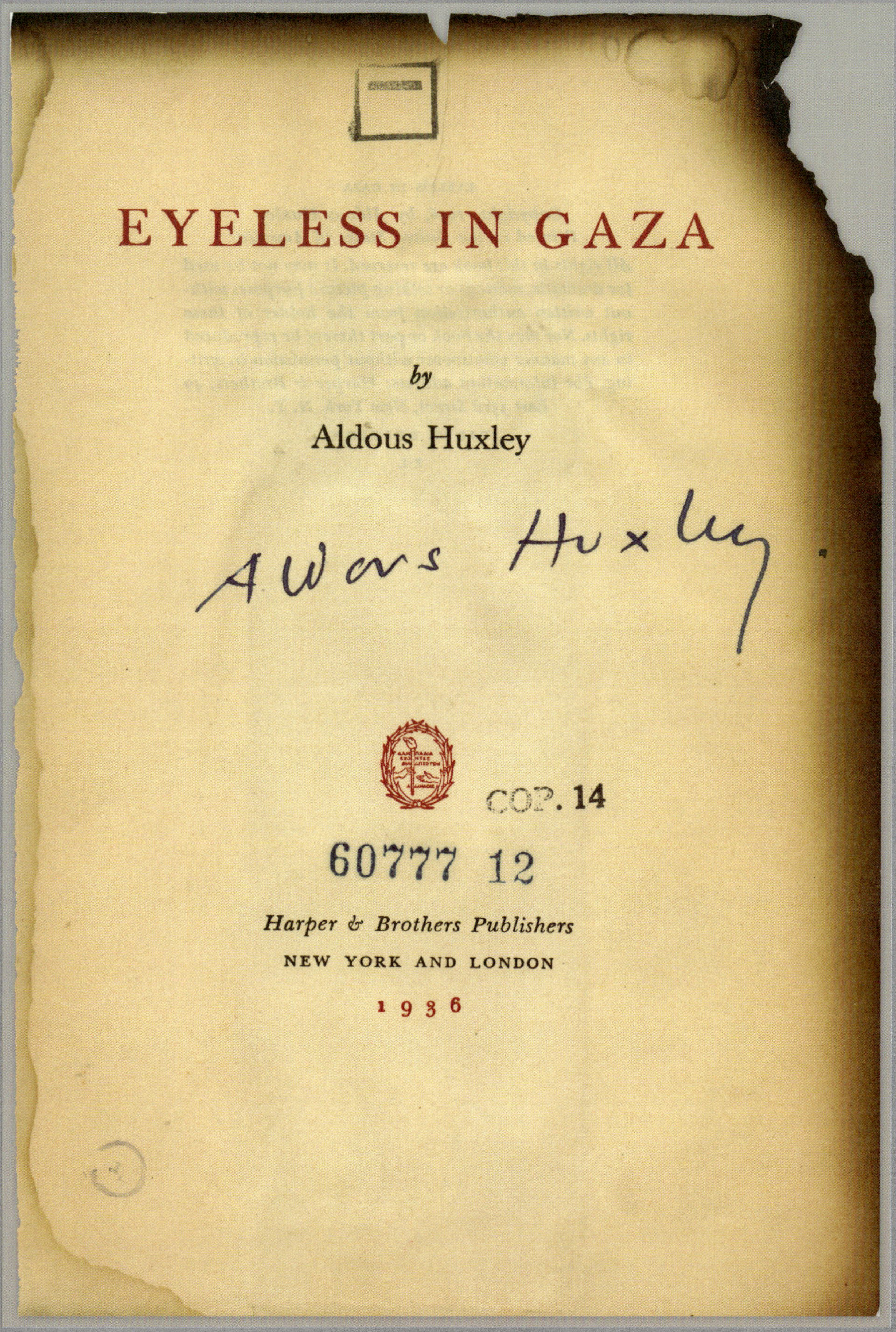
EYELESS IN GAZA

by

Aldous Huxley

Aldous Huxley

Harper & Brothers Publishers

NEW YORK AND LONDON

1936

ALDOUS HUXLEY, circa 1936 • *Eyeless in Gaza*

Los Angeles Public Library

Autographs

White sage still grows here
I grew here
Playing in the hillsides,
Oceans and beaches
We still grow here
The Tongva people
Relearning our culture
From seeds
Protected from the assaults
of hatred and ignorance
My ansecestors are burried here
I have seen them
And with every song, every ceremony
I breathe new life, new spirit
Into this place I call HOME

Mercedes Dorame

MERCEDES DORAME, 2018 • White sage still grows here / I grew here / Playing in the hillsides, / Oceans and beaches / We still grow here / The Tongva people / Relearning our culture / From seeds / Protected from the assaults / of hatred and ignorance / My ancestors are buried here / I have seen them / And with every song, every ceremony / I breathe new life, new spirit / Into this place I call HOME

XAVIER CUGAT, 1947

HEITOR VILLA-LOBOS

Los Angeles Public Library

Autographs

LEO LIMÓN, 2019

Cyrus Edwin Dallin, sculptor.

Born Springfield, Utah, Nov. 22, 1861.

This "Medicine Man" is in Fairmount Park,

Philadelphia.

CYRUS E. DALLIN, SCULPTOR 203

THE MEDICINE MAN.

Cyrus E. Dallin
April 25th 1907
Arlington Heights
Mass.

CYRUS EDWIN DALLIN, 1907

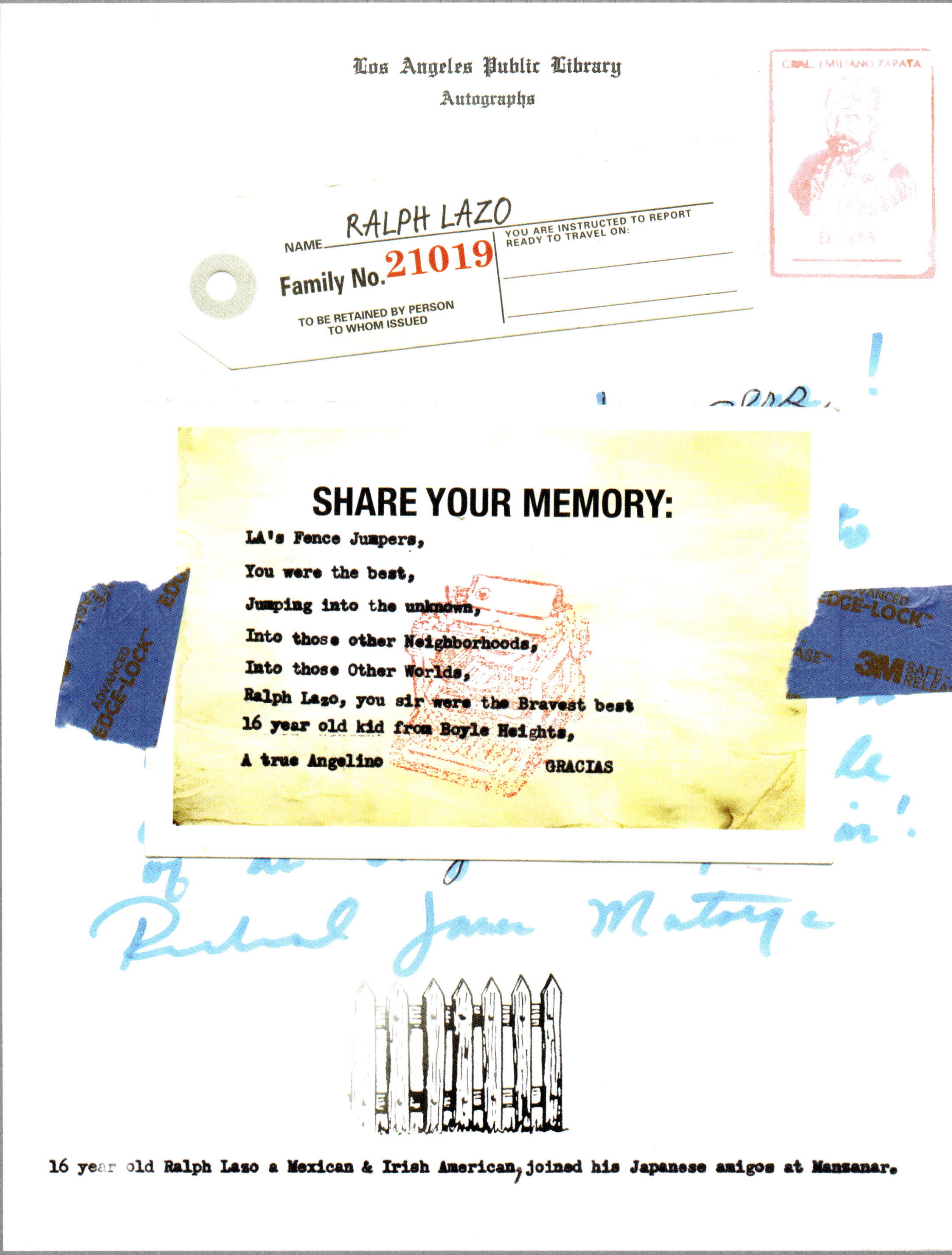

RICHARD MONTOYA, 2019

Los Angeles Public Library

Autographs

It is good to live
in an age when great
and serious problems are
to be solved,

Yours Sincerely
Booker T. Washington
Tuskegee,
Alabama,
Dec. 6, 1906.

BOOKER T. WASHINGTON, 1906 • It is good to live in an age when great and serious problems are to be solved.

WENDY ESCOBAR, 2018 • ***Para mi abuelita La Original Residente de LA***

Los Angeles Public Library

Autographs

Scandinavian poetry, tradition, romance, and history are a fountain of knowledge and delight, which no man can drain dry.

Asgard, Madison
Wisconsin
Jan 23, 1907

R. B. Anderson

RASMUS BJØRN ANDERSON, 1907 • Scandinavian poetry, tradition, romance, and history are a fountain of knowledge and delight, which no man can drain dry.

Los Angeles Public Library

Autographs

HOMEBOY

JOBS NOT JAILS

"IMAGINE A CIRCLE OF COMPASSION

and IMAGINE ...

NO ONE ... STANDING OUTSIDE OF IT."

Gregory J. Boyle

GREGORY J. BOYLE, 2019

Los Angeles Public Library

Autographs

The Ideal

Something I may not win attracts me ever, –
Something elusive yet supremely fair,
Thrills me with gladness, but contents me never,
Fills me with sadness, yet forbids despair.

It blossoms just beyond the paths I follow,
It shines beyond the farthest stars I see,
It echoes faint from ocean caverns hollow,
And from the land of dreams it beckons me.

It calls, and all my best, with joyful feeling
Essays to reach it as I make reply;
I feel its sweetness o'er my spirit stealing; –
Yet know ere I attain it I must die!

Florence Earle Coates

Philadelphia
February 12/07

FLORENCE EARLE COATES, 1907 • Something I may not win attracts me ever, / Something elusive, yet supremely fair, / Thrills me with gladness, but contents me never, / Fills me with sadness, yet forbids despair. // It blossoms just beyond the paths I follow, / It shines beyond the farthest stars I see, / It echoes faint from ocean caverns hollow, / And from the land of dreams it beckons me. // It calls, and all my best, with joyful feeling, / Essays to reach it as I make reply; / I feel its sweetness o'er my spirit stealing, / Yet know ere I attain it I must die!

SEBASTIAN S. PETERSEN, 2018

EDMUND WALLER "TED" GALE, early 1900s

Neil Armstrong, Edwin Aldrin, Jr., Michael Collins: We are with you all the way!

THE BROWNS, STEPHEN, PHIL, TERRY, STEPH, CINDIE AND JENNIE

Mr. & Mrs. Robert Patton

Barbra Perei

Ceola Lavon Kaufman
Nathan Bernard Kaufman

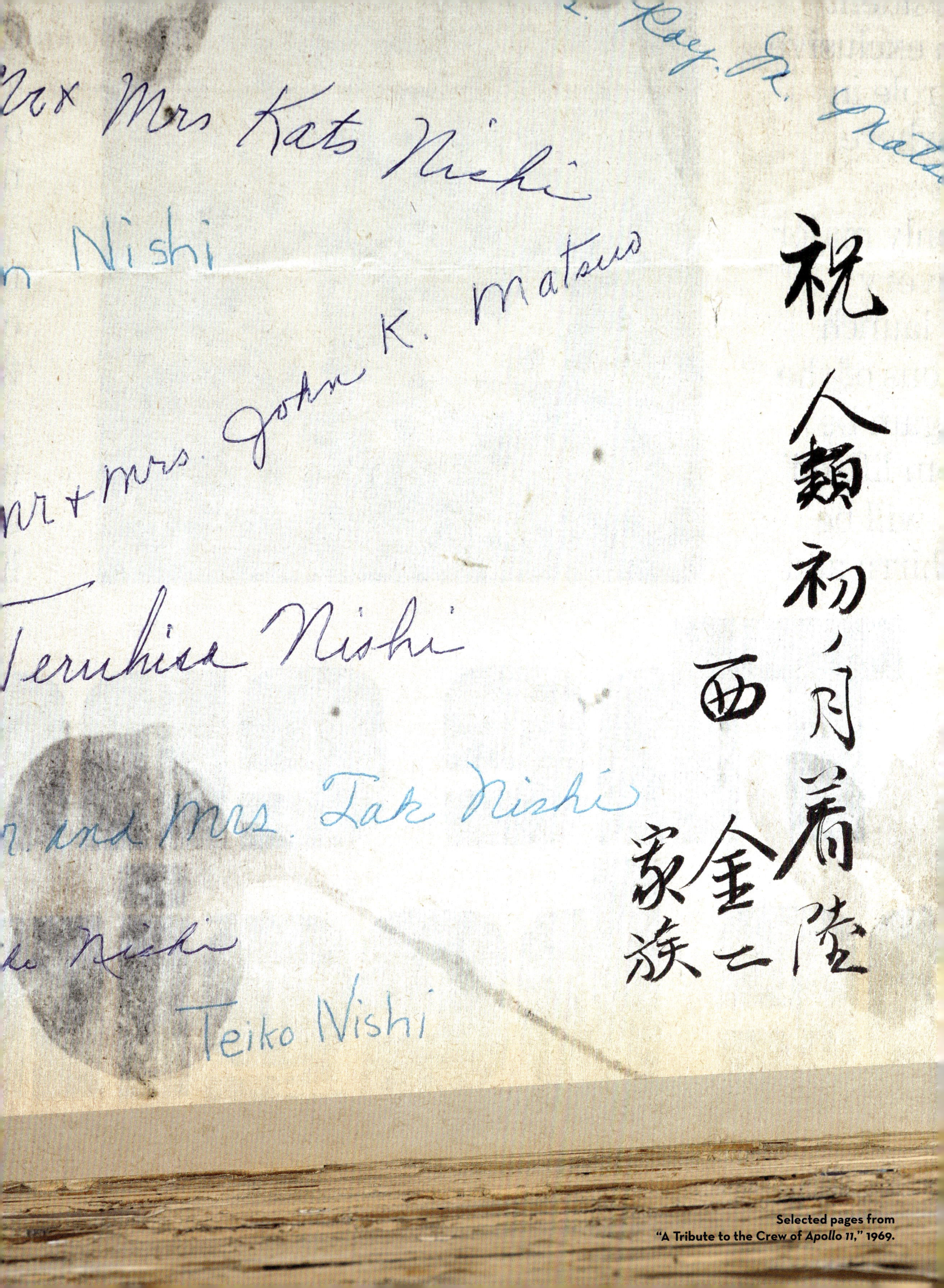
祝
人類初ノ月着陸
西金二
家族

...Ray Jr. Matsu...
Mr & Mrs Kats Nishi
...n Nishi
mr + mrs. John K. Matsuo
Teruhisa Nishi
...r. and Mrs. Tak Nishi
...ko Nishi
Teiko Nishi

Selected pages from "A Tribute to the Crew of *Apollo 11*," 1969.

Los Angeles Public Library

Autographs

(The Poet Scout's Creed)

SUNSHINE

I never like to see a man a 'rastlin' with the dumps
'Cause in the game of life he doesn't always catch the trumps;
But I can always cotton to a free and easy cuss
As takes his dose, and thanks the Lord it isn't any wuss.
There ain't no use o' kickin' and swearin' at your luck,
Yer can't correct the trouble mor'n you can drown a duck.
Remember, when beneath the load your sufferin' head is bowed,
That God 'ill sprinkle sunshine in the trail of every cloud.

If you should see a fellow-man with trouble's flag unfurled,
And lookin' like he didn't have a friend in all the world,
Go up and slap him on the back, and holler "how'd you do,"
And grasp his hand so warm he'll know he has a friend in you.
Then ax him what's a-hurtin' 'im, and laugh his cares away,
And tell him that the darkest night is just afore the day.
Don't talk in graveyard palaver, but say it right out loud,
That God 'ill sprinkle sunshine in the trail of every cloud.

This world at best is but a hash of pleasure and of pain.
Some days are bright and sunny, and some all sloshed with rain.
And that's just how it ought to be, for when the clouds roll by,
We'll know just how to 'preciate the bright and smilin' sky.
So learn to take it as it comes, and don't sweat at the pores
Because the Lord's opinion doesn't coincide with yours;
But always keep rememberin' when cares your path enshroud,
That God has lots of sunshine to spill behind the cloud,

When a bit of sunshine hits ye,
After passing of a cloud,
When a fit of laughter gits ye
An' ye'r spine is feelin' proud,
Don't fergit to up and fling it
At a soul that's feelin' blue,
For the minit that ye sling it
It's a boomerang to you.

What Do I Know?

What do I know? Poor little me,
I need a microscope to see
What I do know;
The overflow
Of nature's riches, all aglow
And sparkling with the stars and dew,
I only know beyond the blue
I cannot see.
Poor little me.
What do I know? I know but this:—
I know my ignorance is bliss
Most wisely planned.
I understand
That tow'ring pines and mountains grand
Are dear and beautiful to me;
Beyond their peaks I cannot see,
But God is there,
And everywhere
And this is good enough for me.

My 60th Birth day
Mar. 4th 1907

And After All

What are you What am I?
But a Stew and a fry,
A broyle and a Siz,
A Scramble for Biz,
And Six feete of Earth
When we die.

John Wallace Crawford
"Capt. Jack"

Once a Good Scout
Now, a poor Poet.
June. "An Thats No lie".

JOHN WALLACE CRAWFORD, "CAPTAIN JACK," 1907 • "And After All" What are you What am I / But a Stew and a fry, / A broyle and a Siz, A Scramble for Biz, / And Six feete of Earth / When we die

Los Angeles Public Library
Autographs

Cheech
18

CHEECH MARIN, 2018

Los Angeles Public Library

Autographs

"So long as human hearts yearn for consolation, so long as human spirits feel the impulse of a diviner life, so long will they find in art a refuge and seek it as a fountain of life; so long also will be found in the world seers and poets and painters whose chief joy in life is to interpret the sweet spirit of the master's music". (from "The Building of a Picture")

Wm. L. Judson

WILLIAM LEES JUDSON, early 1900s • So long as human hearts yearn for consolation, so long as human spirits feel the impulse of a diviner life, so long will they find in art a refuge and seek it as a fountain of life; so long also will be found in the world peers and poets and painters whose chief joy in life is to interpret the sweet spirit of the master's music.

Los Angeles Public Library
Autographs

October 10, 2018

Two of the least appreciated words in the English language are "over" and "next." When something is over it is over and we are on to next. And if there was a hammock between those two words, that hammock would be the best definition I know of living in the moment.

Norman Lear

Norman Lear

NORMAN LEAR, 2018

Los Angeles Public Library

Autographs

If to dream, with some faith, of a time when the productive power of all men will be raised to a high and virtually equal level, when all will have abundance, when there will be none enervatingly rich and none enervatingly poor, when there will be no distinctions of class, but when all will belong to the highest class, and when voters will be so wise, and officials so honest and capable, that all natural monopolies can be left to the management of the state — if to dream and hope and work for such a time, is to be a socialist, I am a socialist. Moreover, if to believe that in such a time, government, so far as it means punishment and repression, will be superfluous and disappear, is to be an anarchist, I am an anarchist. But to believe that such a time will be reached by us or our children or our grandchildren, is simply to be a lunatic; and in that sense the socialist and the anarchist are simply lunatics.

Sturmsee. III.Edn.,pp.205-7. Henry Holt.

HENRY HOLT, early 1900s

FRIENDS OF GRIFFITH PARK, 2018 • greetings from Griffith Park's resident puma ... P-22 in Griffith Park since 2012

ESTO ONE, 2018

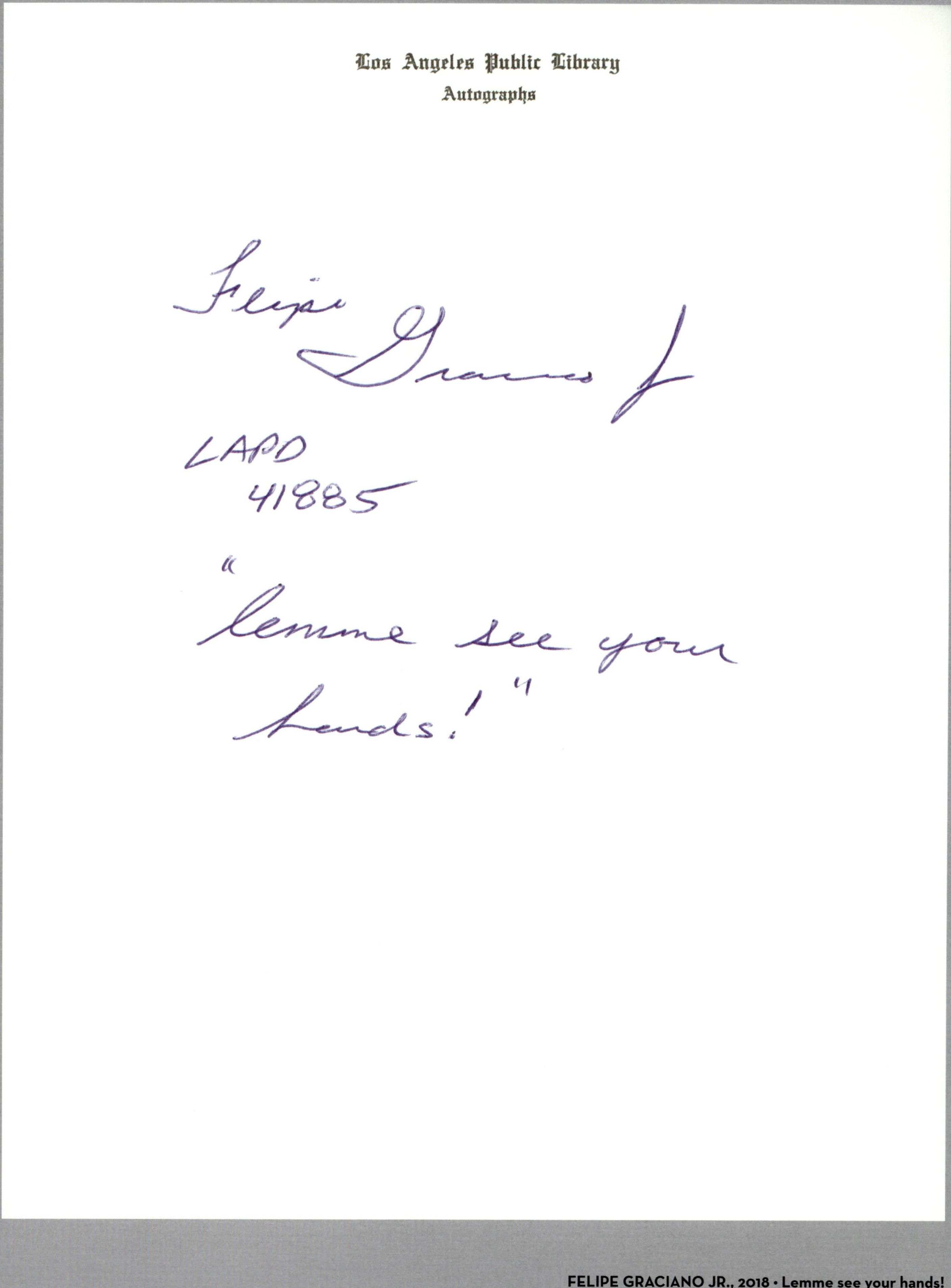
Los Angeles Public Library
Autographs

Felipe Graciano Jr

LAPD
41885

"lemme see your hands!"

FELIPE GRACIANO JR., 2018 • Lemme see your hands!

Los Angeles Public Library

Autographs

Dear Los Angeles,

I've had a love affair with you since my youth. You captivated my soul in ways that I cannot describe. Thank you for being so mysterious and wise and wonderful. Thank you for showing me beauty and wonder and weirdness. I am glad in the years that have passed, I have learned your ways and am so comfortable in all of you. Thank you for providing the traffic that made my mother show me the alternate routes. Thank you for providing those murals along your edges that always make me smile and let me know that my journey home is halfway through. Thank you for your mountains, Beaches and neighborhoods. Thank you for attracting such a variety of people that fills in all of your eccelctic corners. I Love you Los Angeles, and with every day that passes, I grow to love you more.

with all the ♡ in my heart,

IRERI ESPINOZA-TABOADA, 2018

HENRY RANKIN POORE, early 1900s • Art demands that Man shall reedit Nature over his own signature

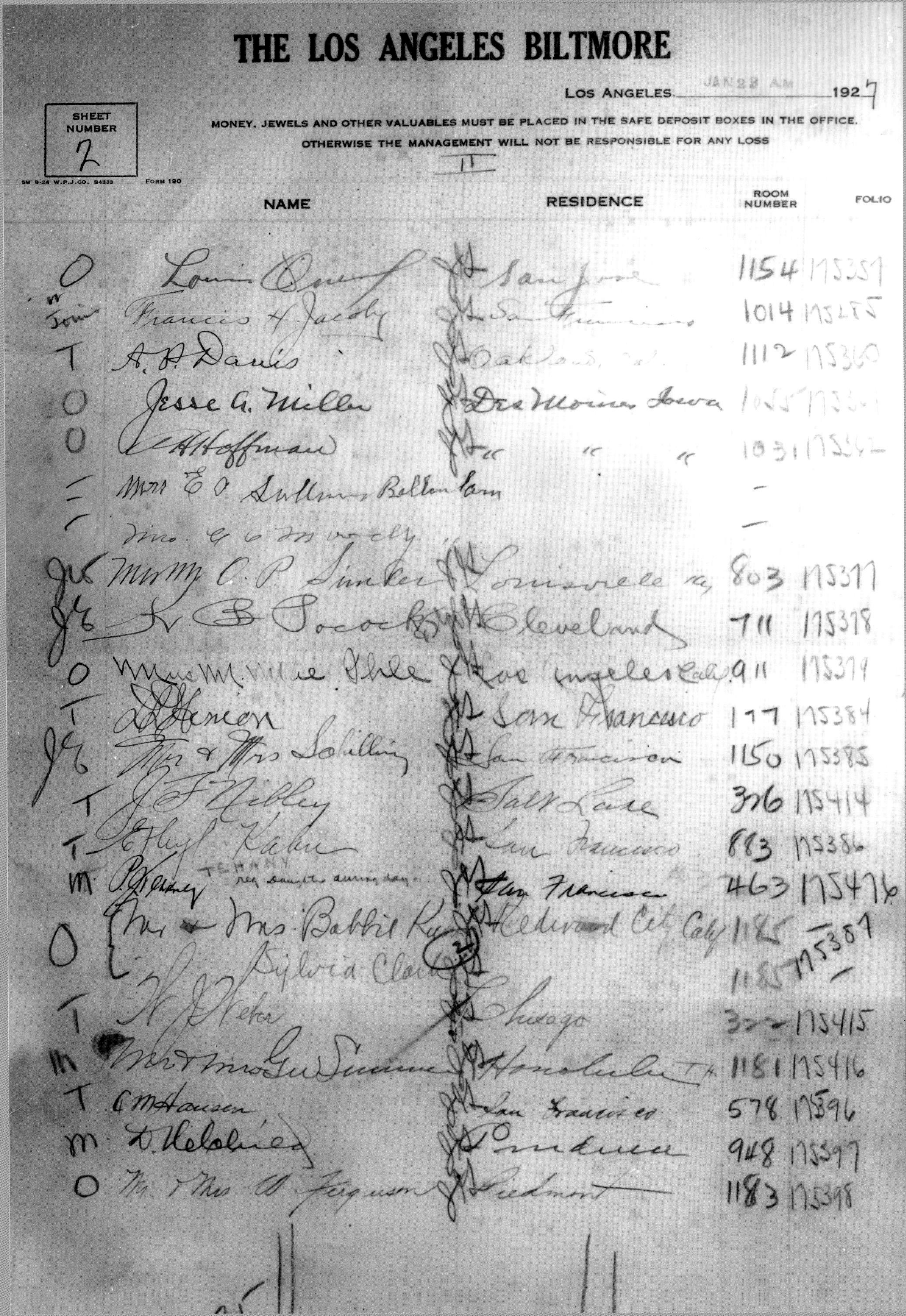

THE LOS ANGELES BILTMORE

LOS ANGELES. ______ 192__

SHEET NUMBER

MONEY, JEWELS AND OTHER VALUABLES MUST BE PLACED IN THE SAFE DEPOSIT BOXES IN THE OFFICE. OTHERWISE THE MANAGEMENT WILL NOT BE RESPONSIBLE FOR ANY LOSS

FORM 190

NAME	RESIDENCE	ROOM NUMBER	FOLIO

The guest register from the Los Angeles Biltmore in downtown Los Angeles, 1927.

Los Angeles Public Library
Autographs

Naima J. Keith

NAIMA J. KEITH, 2018

Los Angeles Public Library

Autographs

M. A. B.

Mary A. Bartow

Los Angeles

October 11, 1906.

MARY A. BARTOW, 1906

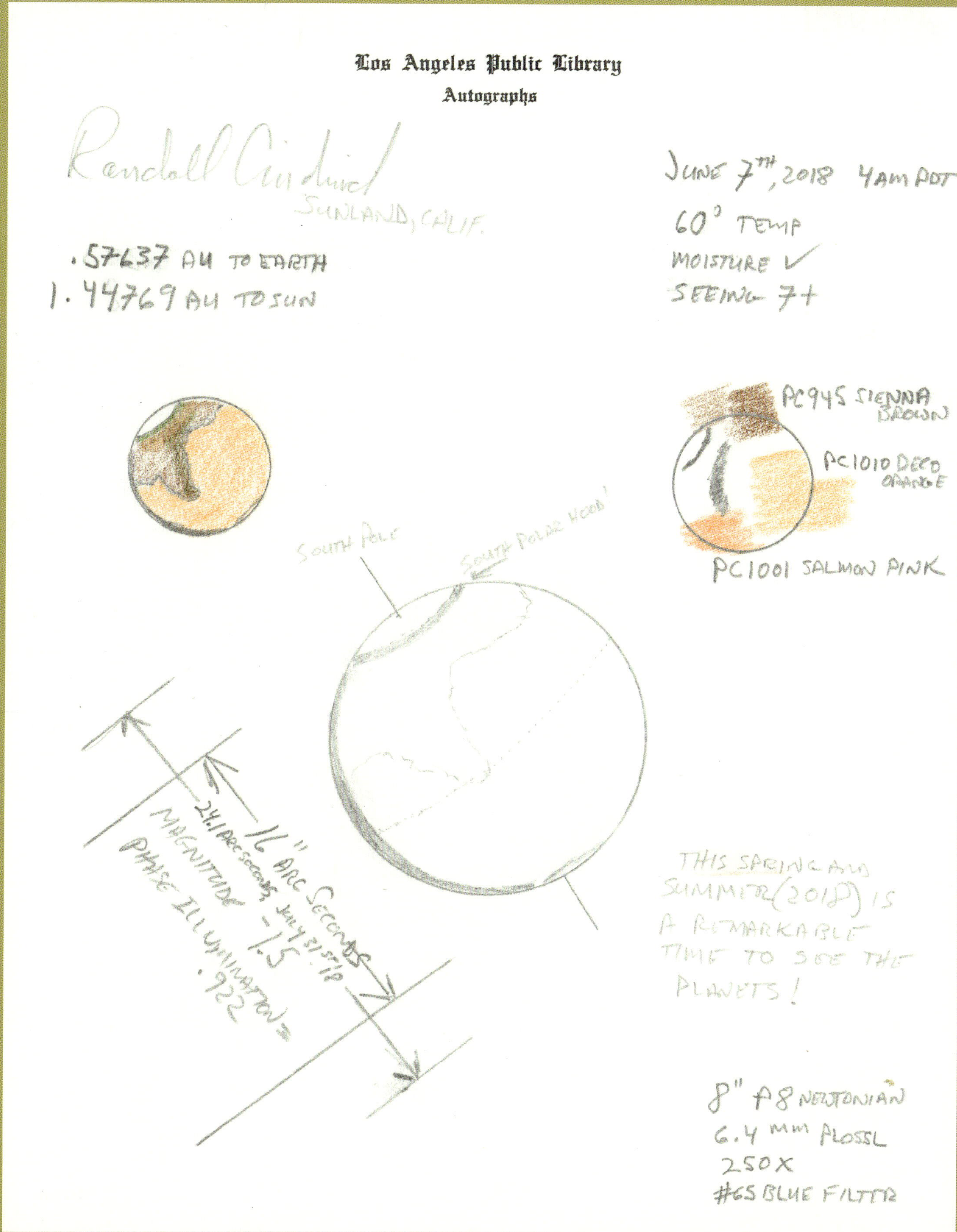

RANDALL CINDRICH, 2018 • This spring and summer (2018) is a remarkable time to see the planets!

Los Angeles Public Library

Autographs

Yours as ever

Wm Keith

WILLIAM KEITH, early 1900s • Yours as ever. The page includes a cyanotype by Charles Lummis.

Los Angeles Public Library

Autographs

CAMARILLO, CA 1 AUG 2018

I WAS BORN IN A LITTLE VILLAGE OF 13 HOUSES IN GUATEMALA, CENTRAL AMERICA.

AT THE AGE OF 8 MY PARENTS MOVE ME TO GUATEMALA CITY. WE WHERE VERY POOR, I ATTENDED SCHOOL IN THE MORNING AND IN THE AFTERNOON I WAS A SHOESHINE BOY. A 8 YEARS OLD BOY ALONE IN THE BIG CITY, I ASKED FOR FOOD LEFT OVER TO FEED MY SIBLINGS, WHEN I DIDN'T GET ENOUGH LEFTOVERS, I LOOKED FOR FOOD IN THE LOCAL TRASH DUMP WHERE SOMETIMES I HAD TO FIGHT WITH STREET DOGS FOR FOOD. I SURVIVED THE STREETS.

WE HAD 36 YEARS OF CIVIL WAR IN GUATEMALA. I DECIDED TO TRAVEL TO UNITED STATES AND SEE IF I CAN/WOULD ACHIEVE THE AMERICAN DREAM.

I ARRIVED IN CALIFORNIA AT THE AGE OF 21 WITH (1981) ONLY 6 GRADE OF SCHOOLING, NO IMMIGRATION DOCUMENTS, NO RELATIVES AND NO ENGLISH. I WORKED ON ALL KIND OF JOBS AS DISHWASHER, PAINTER, WELDER, GARDENER ETC. I STARTED AS A GARDENER AT THE MUSEUM WITH ONE OF THE LARGEST BIRD EGG COLLECTION IN THE WORLD. AT NIGH AFTER WORK I WENT TO SCHOOL AND NOW I AM A BIOLOGIST IN CHARGE OF THE MUSEUM WHERE I STARTED AS A GARDENER. I AM ALSO A WRITER AUTHOR OF THE BOOK EL LUSTRADOR (THE SHOESHINE BOY) AND THE ADVENTURES OF RENÉ CORADO THE SHOESHINE BOY.

RENÉ CORADO
EL LUSTRADOR

RENÉ CORADO, EL LUSTRADOR, 2018

CHRIS HIATT, 2018

Los Angeles Public Library
Autographs

October 18, 2018

To my beloved City of Los Angeles,

Thank you for accepting me warmly upon my arrival from Pennsylvania in 1957. Your being home to people of all nationalities, colors and religions made it easy for me to simply be myself, a second generation American of Italian/Arab descent. In Los Angeles, I was not considered different and unwelcome but rather interesting and somewhat mysterious, and you provided me with the unique education and mentoring needed to achieve my goals.

In the years that followed, I traveled alone to remote parts of the Middle East on a quest to film and record the traditional music and dances that were disappearing from these regions. Although work has taken me to fascinating cities all over the world, it is always a joy to return home to you. There is no place I would prefer to be, and each day I feel grateful to live in this beautiful City of the Angels.

Your loving denizen,

Aisha Ali

AISHA ALI, 2018

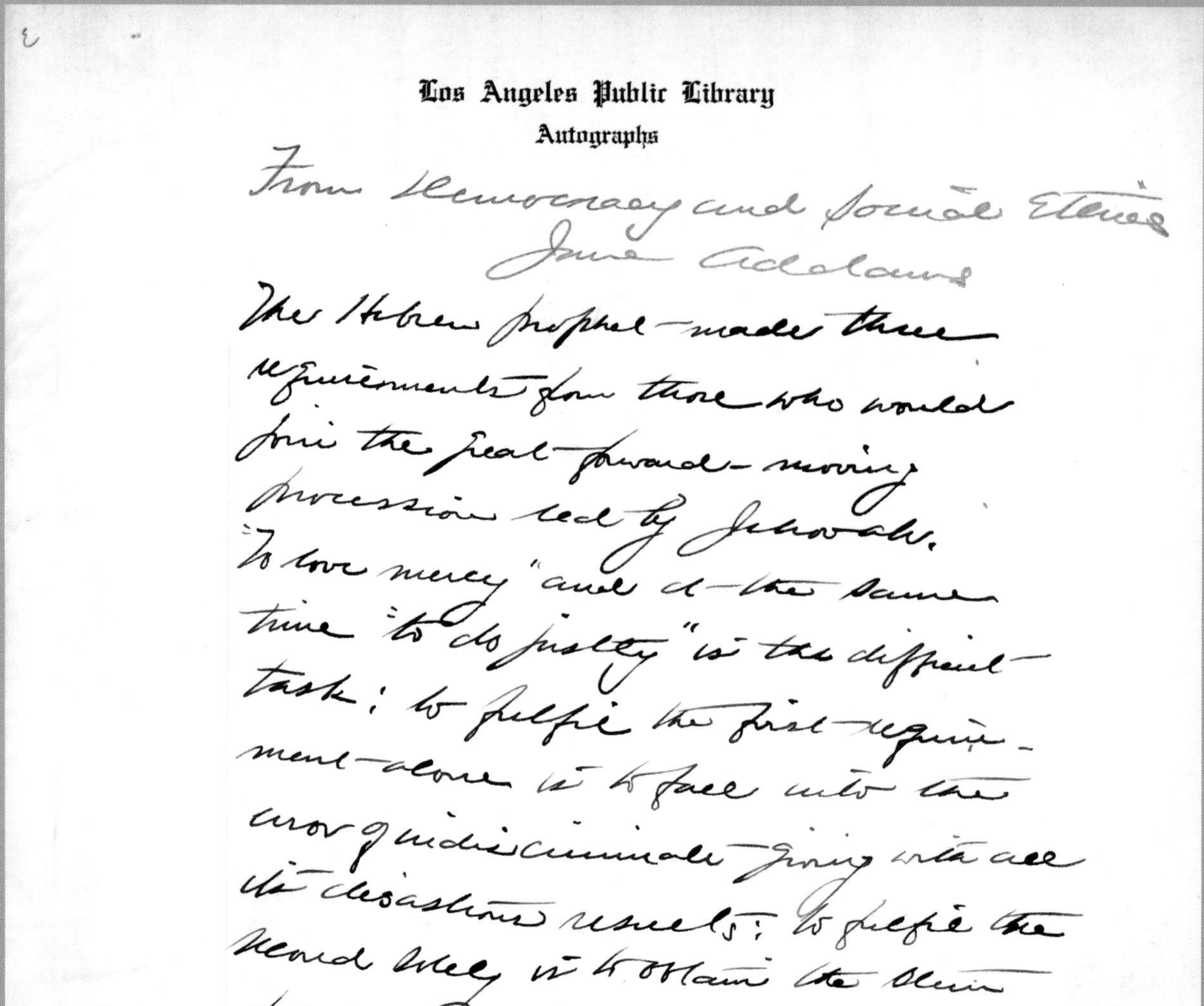

Los Angeles Public Library
Autographs

From "Democracy and Social Ethics"
Jane Addams

The Hebrew prophet made three requirements from those who would join the great forward-moving procession led by Jehovah. "To love mercy" and at the same time "to do justly" is the difficult task; to fulfil the first requirement alone is to fall into the error of indiscriminate giving with all its disastrous results; to fulfil the second solely is to obtain the stern policy of withholding. ********

It may be that the combination of the two can never be attained save as we fulfil still the third requirement = "to walk humbly with God" which may be to walk for many dreary miles beside the lowliest of His creatures, not even in that peace of mind which the company of the humble is supposed to afford but rather with the pangs and throes to which the poor human understanding is subjected when it attempts to comprehend the meaning of life.

JANE ADDAMS, early 1900s • **The Hebrew prophet made three requirements from those who would join the great forward-moving procession led by Jehovah. "To love mercy" and at the same time "to do justly" is the difficult task; to fulfil the first requirement alone is to fall into the error of indiscriminate giving with all its disastrous results; to fulfil the second solely is to obtain the stern policy of withholding. It may be that the combination of the two can never be attained save as we fulfil still the third requirement—"to walk humbly with God," which may mean to walk for many dreary miles beside the lowliest of His creatures, not even in that peace of mind which the company of the humble is popularly supposed to afford but rather with the pangs and throes to which the poor human understanding is subjected whenever it attempts to comprehend the meaning of life.**

ALEX COHEN, 2018

Los Angeles Public Library
Autographs

Andante.

Marie Azpiroz

Nov. 29, 1909
Los Angeles. Cal.

MARIE AZPIROZ, 1909

Los Angeles Public Library

Autographs

I wrote a novel in this library
in 1969. Sold it too! (18 years later)

Walter Koenig

WALTER KOENIG, 2018 • I wrote a novel in this library in 1969. Sold it too! (18 years later)

TOMMY KOULAX

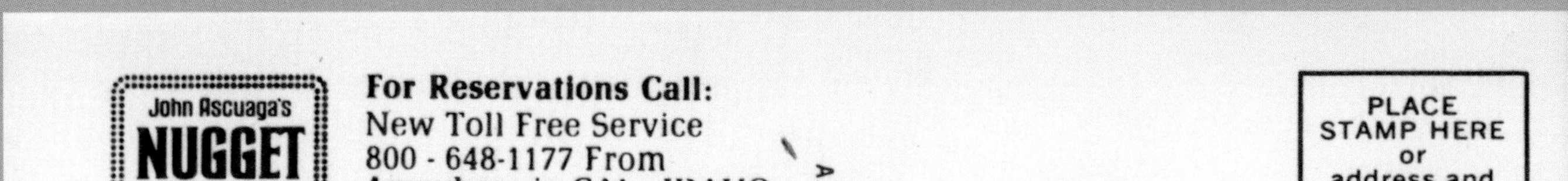

LIBERACE, 1971

Los Angeles Public Library

Autographs

X: Gary Leonard

GARY LEONARD, 2019

MISTER CARTOON, 2019

TAT2
LA
MR. CARTOON

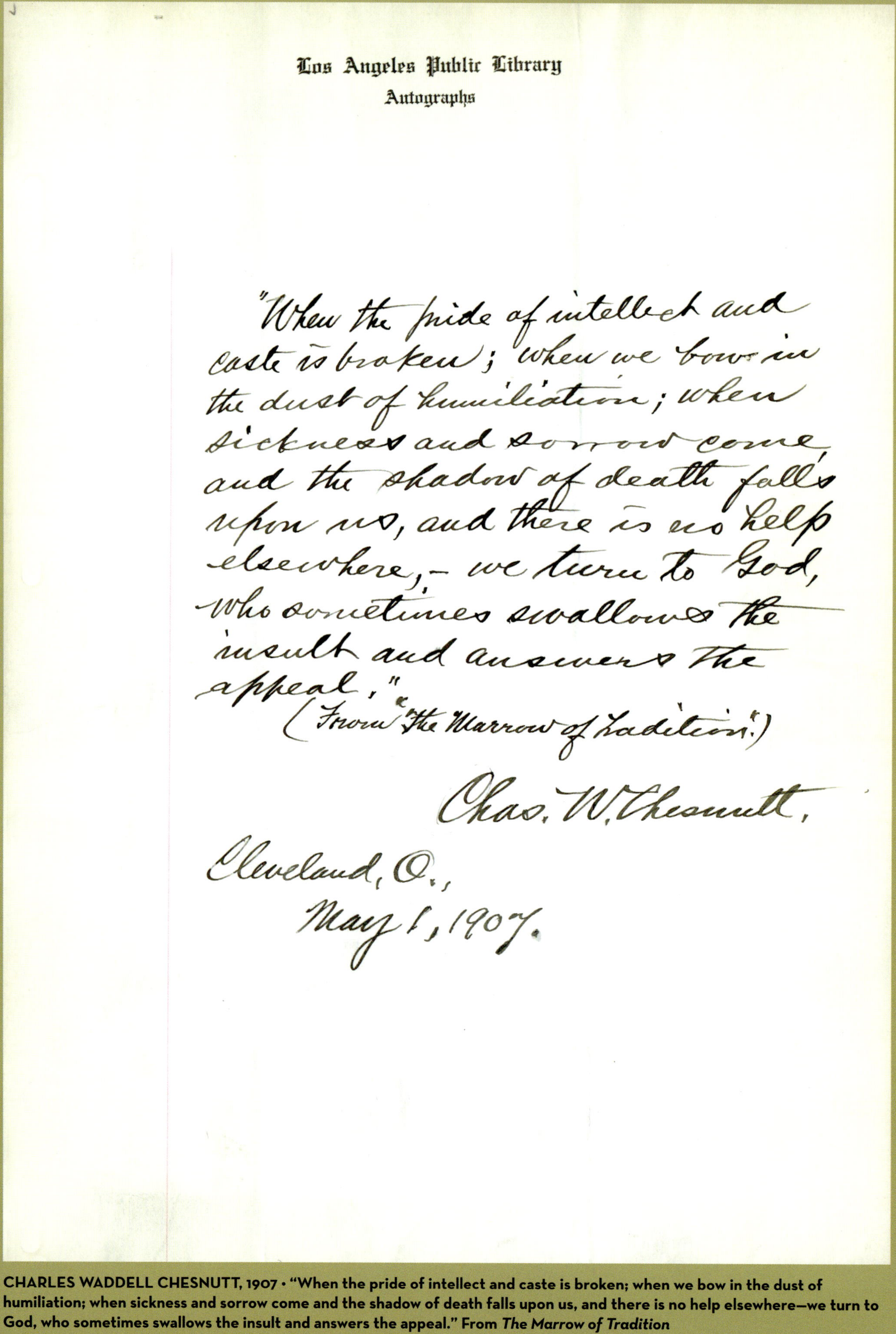

Los Angeles Public Library

Autographs

"When the pride of intellect and caste is broken; when we bow in the dust of humiliation; when sickness and sorrow come, and the shadow of death falls upon us, and there is no help elsewhere,— we turn to God, who sometimes swallows the insult and answers the appeal."

(From "The Marrow of Tradition.")

Chas. W. Chesnutt.

Cleveland, O.,

May 1, 1907.

CHARLES WADDELL CHESNUTT, 1907 • "When the pride of intellect and caste is broken; when we bow in the dust of humiliation; when sickness and sorrow come and the shadow of death falls upon us, and there is no help elsewhere—we turn to God, who sometimes swallows the insult and answers the appeal." From *The Marrow of Tradition*

Los Angeles Public Library

Autographs

Surely we cannot be the only ones awake, even if we are the only ones with a single lamp lit. No, we cannot be alone! Thousands more must be staring into darkness like us, gripped by scandalous thoughts, extravagant hopes, and forbidden plots. We lie in wait for the right moment and the just cause, which, at this moment, is simply wanting to live. And even as we write this final sentence, the sentence that will not be revised, we confess to being certain of one and only one thing—we swear to keep, on penalty of death, this one promise:

We will live!

July 14, 2019
Los Angeles
California

VIET THANH NGUYEN, 2019

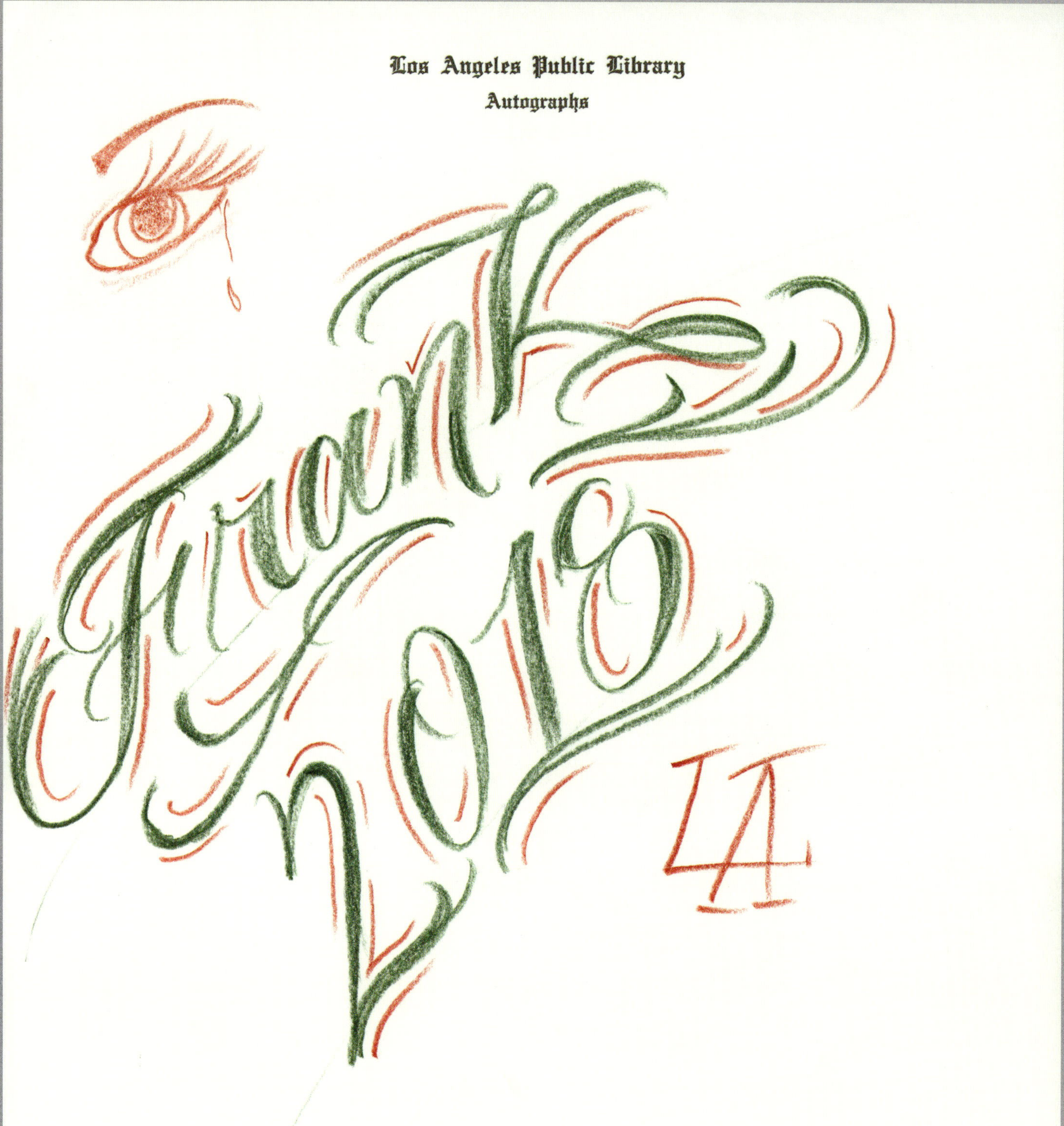

FRANKY DOMINGUEZ, 2018

LOS ANGELES PUBLIC LIBRARY

Autograph Collection

These reduced fac-similes are examples of the generous spirit in which our request is being met.
We have already nearly 800 of these pages.

Los Angeles Public Library
Autographs

HOMER DAVENPORT, 1907

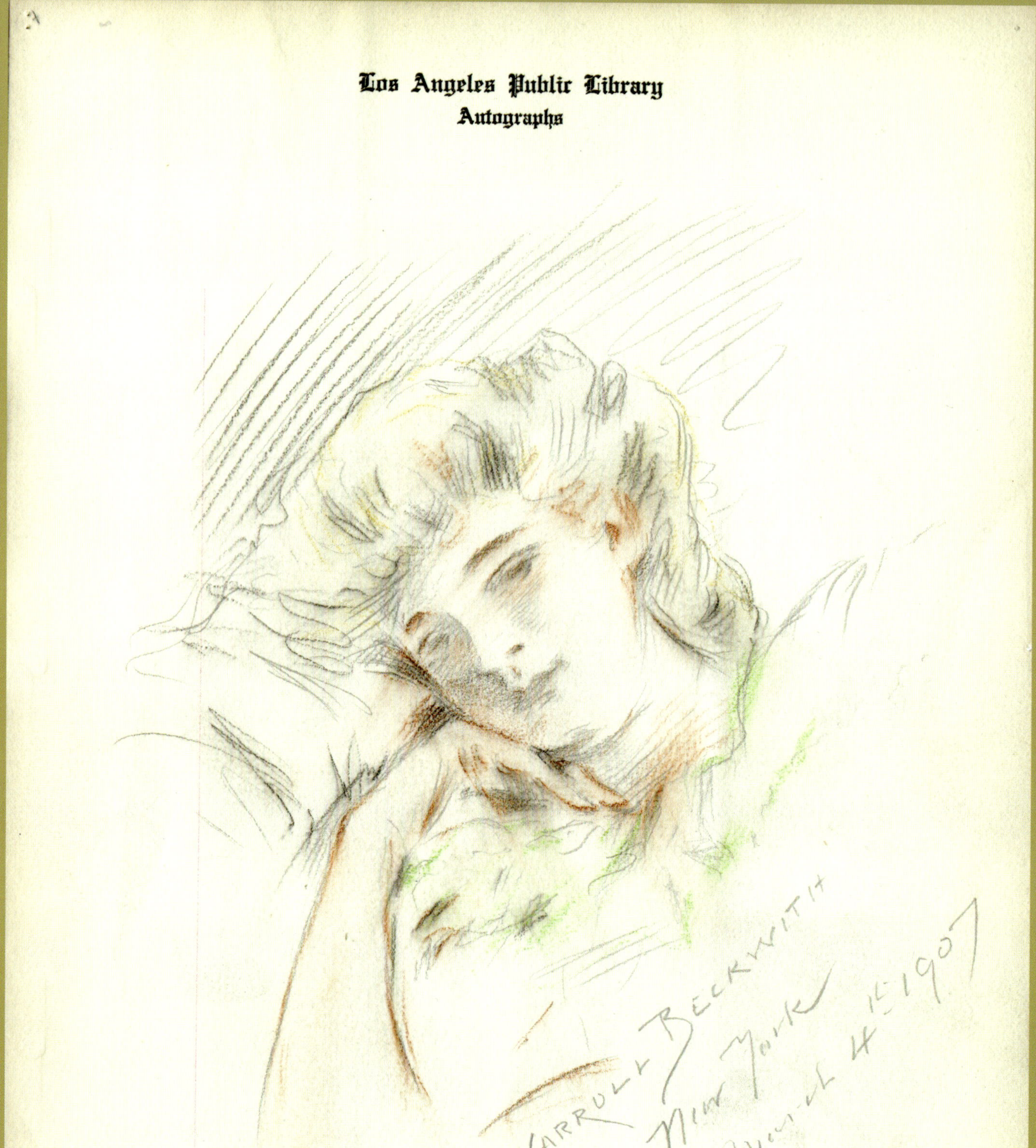

JAMES CARROLL BECKWITH, 1907

Los Angeles Public Library

Autographs

Very sincerely yours
Julia Bracken Wendt
Los Angeles Octob 9, 1906

JULIA BRACKEN WENDT, 1906

Los Angeles Public Library
Autographs

Lynell George

"I often tell people that Los Angeles makes no sense if you talk about it out loud: The land of slowfloat car chases and girls with Mercurochrome hair. So my L.A. exists in my mind, in fragments — a conflation of time, space and reality."
— from "Native to the Place"

(LA to L.A for my family)

LYNELL GEORGE, 2019 • I often tell people that Los Angeles makes no sense if you talk about it out loud: The land of slowfloat car chases and girls with Mercurochrome hair. So my L.A. exists in my mind, in fragments—a conflation of time, space and reality. – from "Native to the Place"

AND THIS THEIR GRIEF

The builders of cities move nearer to God
Than what they believe. This is the secret
Of tall towers towering above the clouds,
Reaching for the sky with a varnished face
Of glass and cement, mocking the earth
Where the indifferent eye rejects the heart
With a false desire.
They cry:
"Give us
The strength to carry an empire of cities;
Give us the hunger to create for pleasure - "
Cry:
"We work
A hard labor through the dark years and suffer
Humiliation, but our tears thaw our sorrow
In the passing of our fears..."

There is a passage into the morning under
Their shadows flowering like a spectre
Of moving heads and clasping hands,
Where the invisible finger points upward
To witness the desultory scene of humdrum
Music, and withdraws into space leaving
Sufficient glory upon wetted brows and lips.

This they never saw and never believed.

They say:
"Our fathers cried for you to come back to us,
And they failed in their eagerness. They shaped
The stone into your image, and bowed to their
Creation believing their prayers. Their way is simple.
But the image is wonderful to the broken body,
The prayers beautiful to the eager ears..."
They never say:
"We cannot pray from our leaping waters filtering
Into the stream of our dream. We can talk to you
In terms of our buildings, roads, bridges.
Any other language is ambiguous - "
Never say:
"We are hard enough to endure the life
That will not let us pass to you, strong enough
To construct immeasurable towers where we engrave
Our desire for you to come back with your music,
And bold enough to crush our dream,
Knowing that you shall never come back
To us waiting under the green grass..."

Not saying this, they girdled their hearts
That will not break of love but pity;
And saying the echo of what they heard
From the hills that will not weep,
They pointed their fingers to the sky
And cried:
"At least we are not dead!"

This is what they said and this they believed.

Carl Bulosan
Los Angeles — Feb. 22, 1936

CARL BULOSAN, 1936

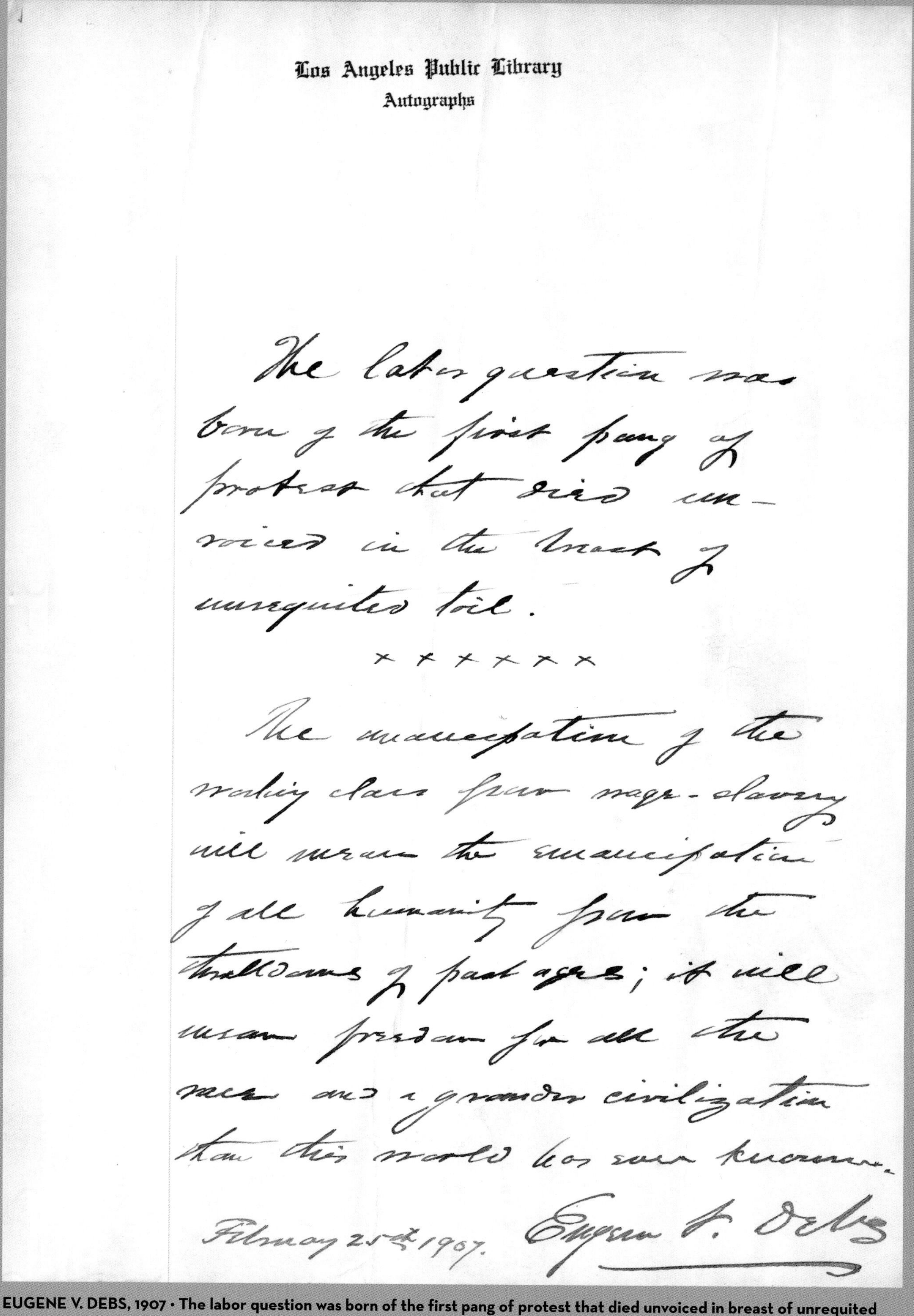

Los Angeles Public Library
Autographs

The labor question was born of the first pang of protest that died unvoiced in the breast of unrequited toil.

× × × × × × ×

The emancipation of the working class from wage-slavery will mean the emancipation of all humanity from the thralldoms of past ages; it will mean freedom for all the races and a grander civilization than this world has ever known.

February 25th 1907. Eugene V. Debs

EUGENE V. DEBS, 1907 • **The labor question was born of the first pang of protest that died unvoiced in breast of unrequited toil. The emancipation of the working class from wage-slavery will mean the emancipation of all humanity from the thralldoms of past ages; it will mean freedom for all the races and a grander civilization than this world has ever known.**

JESUS ESPARZA, 2018 • *Quisieron enterrarnos pero no sabían que éramos semillas.*

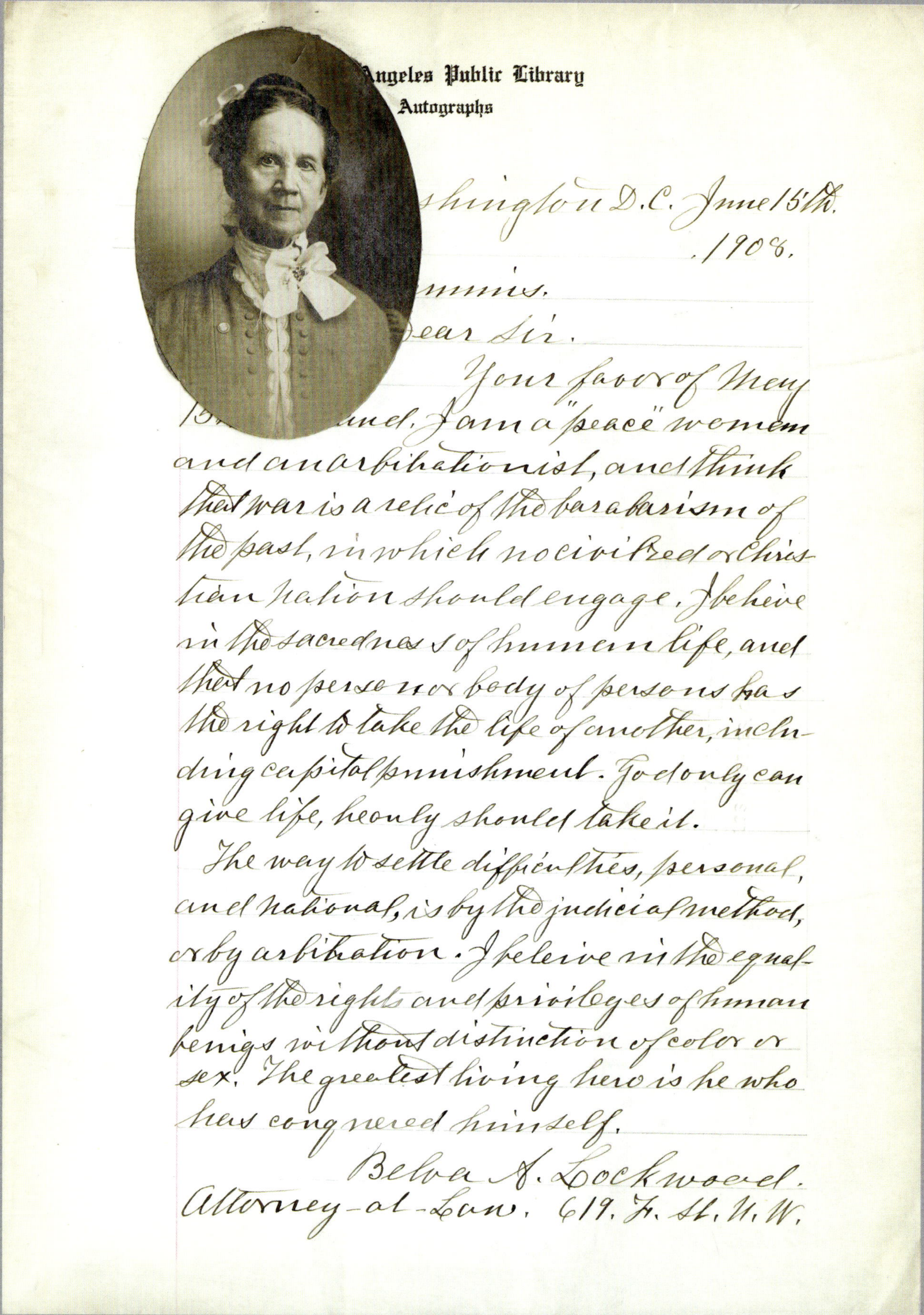

Angeles Public Library
Autographs

shington D.C. June 15th.
1908.

mmis.
Dear Sir.

Your favor of May
1... ...ived. I am a "peace" women
and an arbitrationist, and think
that war is a relic of the barabarism of
the past, in which no civilized or Chris-
tian nation should engage. I beleive
in the sacredness of human life, and
that no perse nor body of persons has
the right to take the life of another, inclu-
ding capital punishment. God only can
give life, he only should take it.

The way to settle difficulties, personal,
and national, is by the judicial method,
or by arbitration. I beleive in the equal-
ity of the rights and privileges of human
beings without distinction of color or
sex. The greatest living hero is he who
has conquered himself.

Belva A. Lockwood.
Attorney-at-Law. 619. F. St. N.W.

BELVA ANN LOCKWOOD, 1908 • I am a "peace" woman and an abolitionist, and think that war is a relic of the barbarism of the past, in which no civilized or Christian nation should engage. I believe in the sacredness of human life, and that no person or body of persons has the right to take the life of another, including capital punishment. God only can give life, he only should take it. The way to settle difficulties, personal, and national, is by the judicial method, or by arbitration. I believe in the equality of the rights and privileges of human beings without distinction of color or sex. The greatest living hero is he who has conquered himself.

MATILDA LOTZ, early 1900s

Los Angeles Public Library

Autographs

=2018=

SANDRA DE LA LOZA, 2018

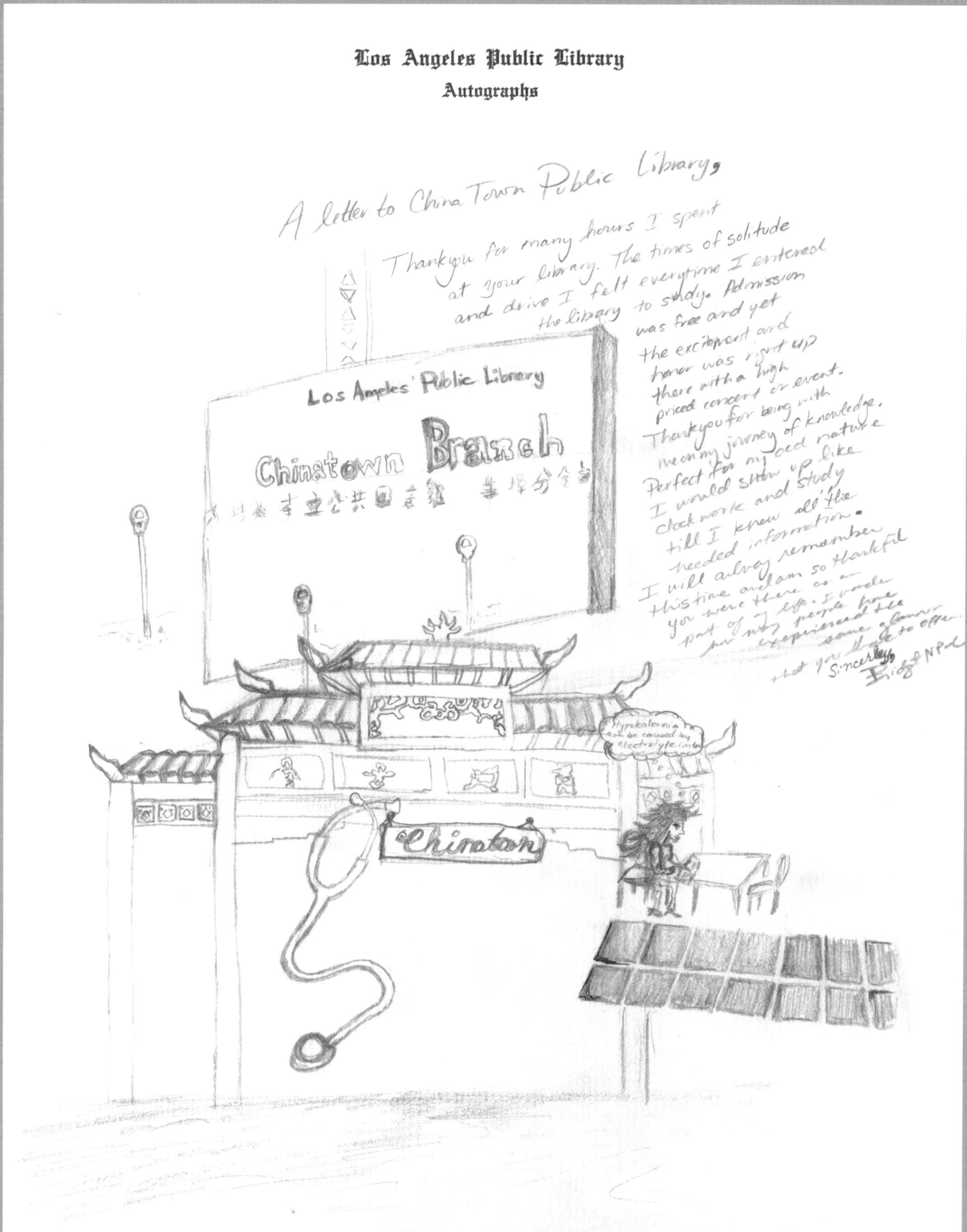

BRIDGET MARRIN, 2018 • A letter to China Town Public Library, Thank you for many hours I spent at your library. The times of solitude and drive I felt everytime I entered the library to study. Admission was free and yet the excitement and honor was right up there with a high priced concert or event. Thank you for being with me on my journey of knowledge. Perfect for my ocd nature. I would show up like clockwork and study till I knew all the needed information. I will always remember this time and am so thankful you were there as a part of my life. I wonder how many people have experienced the same glamour that you have to offer.

Space Station #3 The Spacetts
1. Nancy Leopold
2. Paula Marks
3. Marcia Andersen
4. Anna Garcia
5. Darlene Villanuea
6. Leissa Bankston
7. René Maguill
8. Cindy Stephens
9. Ann Smith
10. Francine Haynes

Space Station #4 Stardust Adorables
1. Mary Jaivits
2. Ann Lucy
3. Maria Bonilla
4. Rebecca Gómez
5. Sue Yegge
6. Janet Anthony
7. Carol William
8. Judy Swain

#6 - "Astro-nuts"
selor
Thunell
NEWHARD
anko
son
Ricksieck
rontz

#8 "MOONMEN"
MSDEN - COUNSELOR
Hill
Vogel
Lakner
Do
Erum
Everett Krupp
an Romero
RYTLEWSKI

FRONE

Anita Sanchez
pher Best

UNI CAMP
900 HILGARD AVE., LOS ANGELES, CALIF.
90024 PHONE (213) 474-1531/879-2100

Neil Armstrong, Edwin Aldrin, Jr, Michael Collins:
We of the younger diabetic session of UCLA's summer camp for children are with you all the way!

Bill Nabor
HEAD COUNSELOR

Martha Berry
Head Counselor

SPACE STATION #9 "ASTRONEEDLES"
Bob Nale
Jim Sykes
Chris Hugunin
Kyle Hadley
Michael Danehy
allen Musselman
John P. Kelley.

SPACE STATION #10 "OUTER LIMITS"
Paul Horsepian
Danny Bullock
Bob Vukich.
Steve Cole
DAVID DOVE
Neil Scott
Richard Hanley
Michael Anthony Lendin
Jeff Clint Potter

SPACE STATION #11 "MARTIAN MARAUDERS"
Bob Hailey
Thomas Frazier
DON CLAGHORN
Don Grisham
Don Hill, Daniels
David Jimenez
Eddie Egan
Jim Nelson
Joe Madrid

Staff
Dan Essin - FLOATER (COUNSELOR)
Alice L. Maguill
Maxine Tanney
Gail Hansen
Vernon C. Maguill
Janet Kerfoot
Mary Gerlach

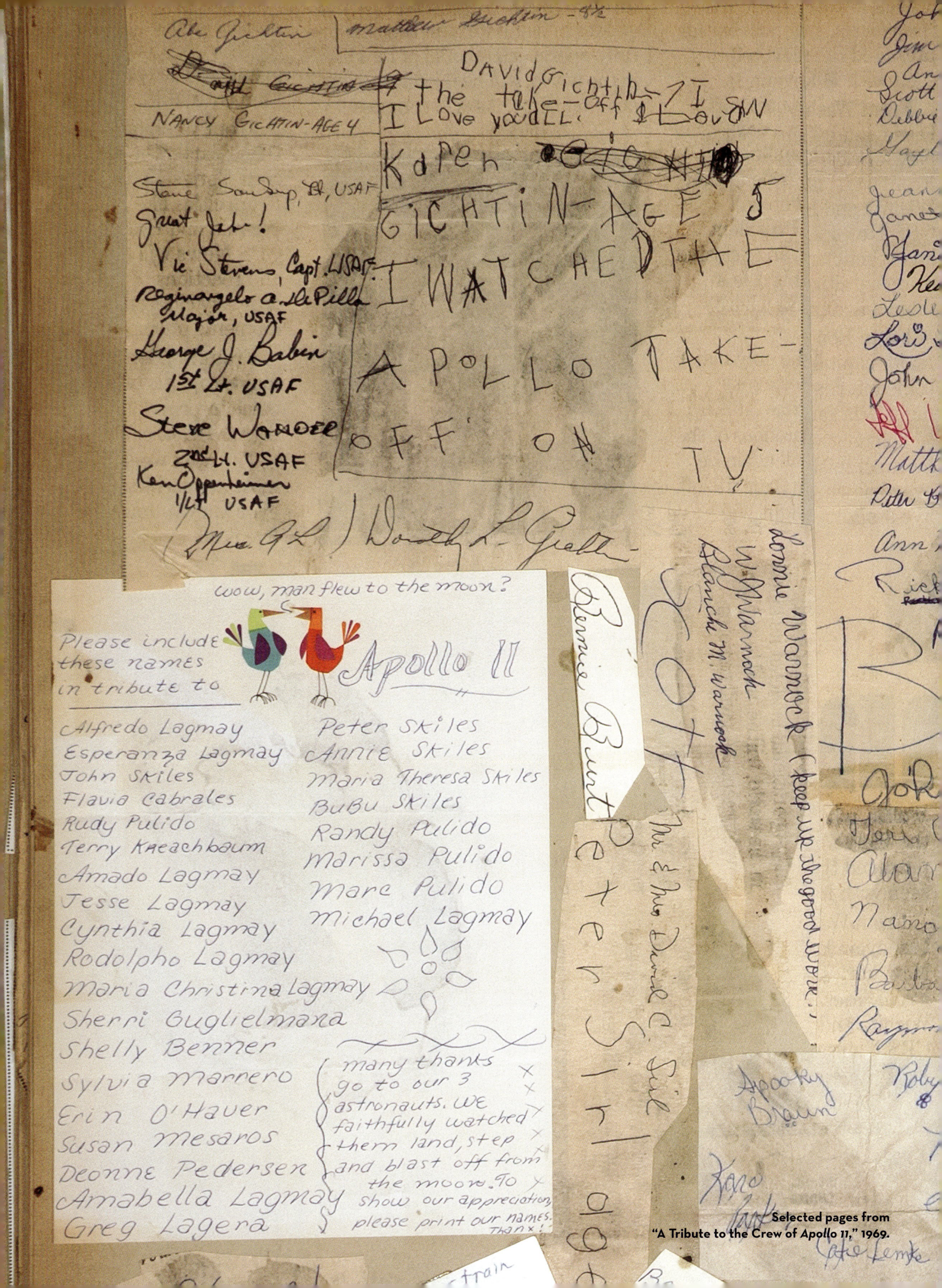

Selected pages from "A Tribute to the Crew of *Apollo 11*," 1969.

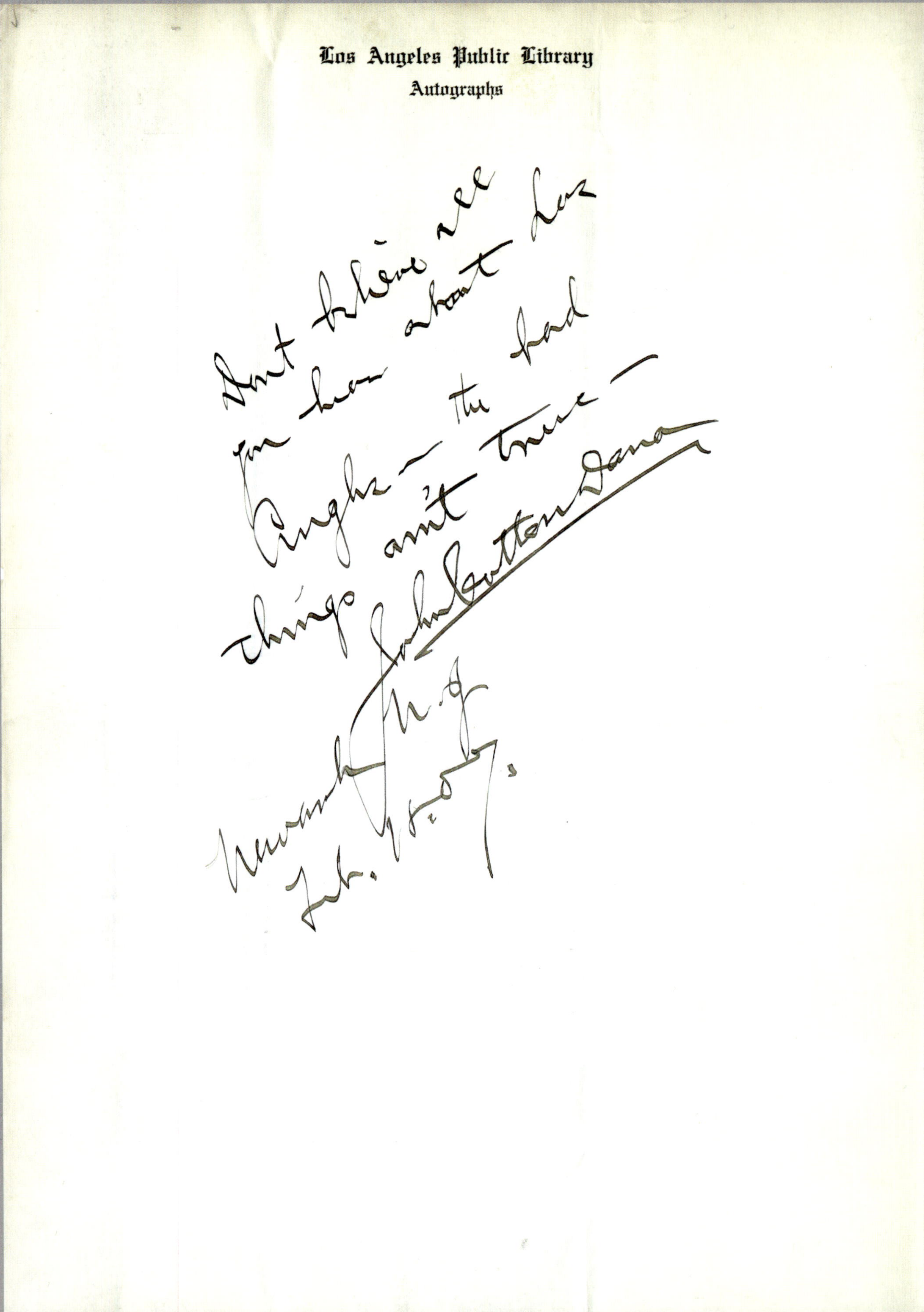

Los Angeles Public Library

Autographs

Dont believe all you hear about Los Angeles — the bad things ain't true —

John Cotton Dana

Newark N.J.

Feb. 1907.

JOHN COTTON DANA, 1907 • Don't believe all you hear about Los Angeles — the bad things ain't true

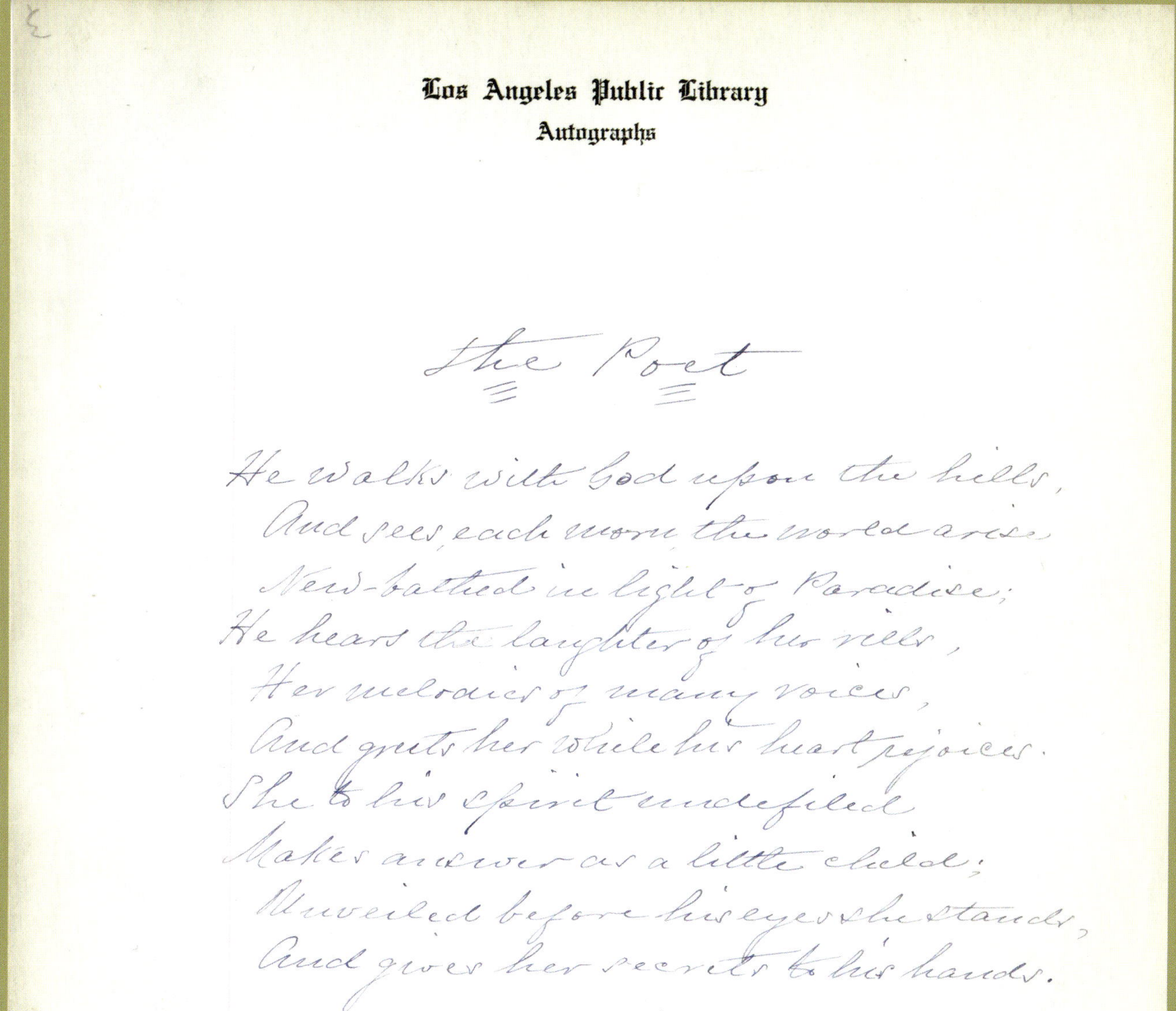

Los Angeles Public Library
Autographs

The Poet

He walks with God upon the hills,
And sees, each morn the world arise
New-bathed in light of Paradise;
He hears the laughter of her rills,
Her melodies of many voices,
And greets her while his heart rejoices.
She to his spirit undefiled
Makes answer as a little child;
Unveiled before his eyes she stands,
And gives her secrets to his hands.

— Ina Coolbrith —

Oct 4, 1906.

INA COOLBRITH, 1906 • **"The Poet" He walks with God upon the hills, / And sees, each morn, the world arise / New-bathed in light of Paradise; / He hears the laughter of her rills, / Her melodies of many voices, / And greets her while his heart rejoices. / She to his spirit undefiled / Makes answer as a little child; / Unveiled before his eyes she stands, / And gives her secrets to his hands.**

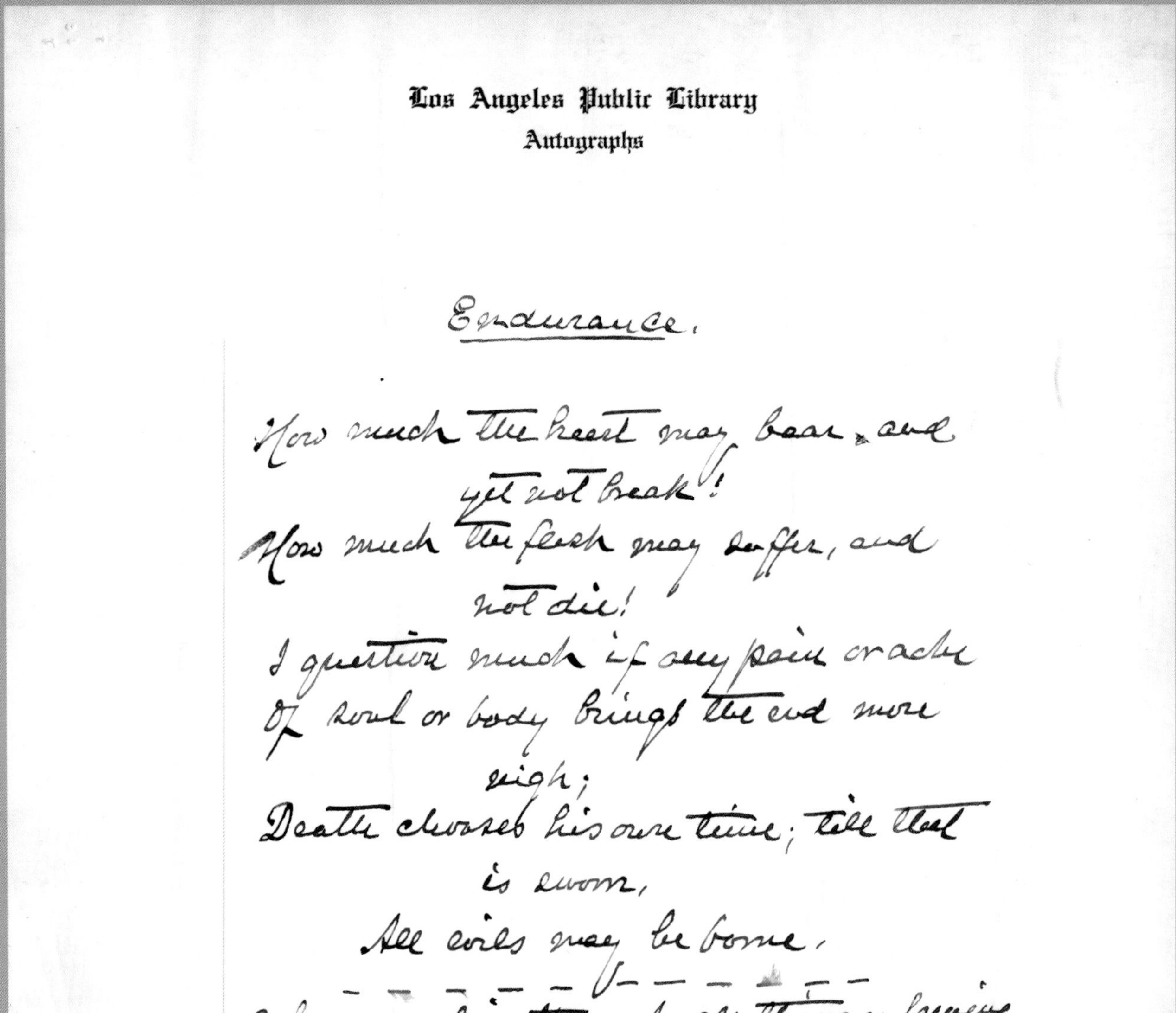
Los Angeles Public Library
Autographs

Endurance.

How much the heart may bear, and yet not break!
How much the flesh may suffer, and not die!
I question much if any pain or ache
Of soul or body brings the end more nigh;
Death chooses his own time; till that is sworn,
All evils may be borne.
Behold, we live through all things; famine, thirst,
Bereavement, pain – all loss and misery,
All woe and sorrow; life inflicts its worst
On soul and body – but we can not die,
Though we be sick, and tired, and faint, and worn;
Lo, all things can be borne!

Elizabeth Akers.

Tuckahoe, New York. January. 1907.

ELIZABETH AKERS, 1907 • "Endurance" How much the heart may bear, and yet not break! / How much the flesh may suffer, and not die! / I question much if any pain or ache — / Of soul or body brings our end more nigh; / Death chooses his own time; till that is sworn, / All evils may be borne. / Behold, we live through all things; famine, thirst, / Bereavement, pain — all loss and misery, / All woe and sorrow; life inflicts its worst / On soul and body — but we cannot die, / Though we be sick, and tired, and faint, and worn; / Lo, all things can be borne!

Los Angeles Public Library

Autographs

The Universe is one force in many manifestations.

There is no time, no space, no matter. The limitations of the human mind give us only glimpses of the great Unity of Nature. Dreams, thoughts, recollections and the imagination annihilate the Conventions of time, space and matter. In the representative neurons of the mind we can go over the battle fields of Napoleon, Ceaser, Hannibal or Ramases; we can walk with Newton, Darwin or Spencer; we can go back aeon by aeon in the geologic record of the earth, or travel with Aladdin or instantly see with our eyes shut, thousands of suns thousands of Light-years away. In thought we annihilate time, space and matter. This fact suggests what future evolution may do for man.

Man is the highest manifestation of the Universe force known to us.

Man is individually enormously small, enormously unimportant.

Each human being is a link in a chain of manifestations of Universe force going on to the Command of higher and higher powers. Man, to make good in the line of evolution to higher things, must improve and must perpetuate the improvements made. There is only one way to do this under the rules of human evidence. This one way is to reproduce and live again by recreation in children.

In this work of creating human beings and in that act recreating ourselves and thus carrying forward toward higher things the trained and educated combination of atoms or electrons called man, Man is of enormous importance. The higher the development of the man, the more tremendously great is the importance of his carrying his evolution forward to greater things by living again in his children and perpetuating, improved, the Universe force called human life.

What life, through the evolution of man is to be, we cannot think. We must believe that it will be wonderfully and in every way higher.

There is but one known way to participate in the higher human and super-human life. This one known way is in perpetuating the life by recreation in children of the improved and highest lives.

It is plain that the highest action of the human being is to improve the highest qualities and powers now possessed. The highest result is to transmit such improved highest powers to a continuation of the life.

Children - the recreation and continuance of the education and improvement of the complex organization of electrons called human life, is of all embracing importance.

Abbot Kinney

ABBOT KINNEY, early 1900s

CARL OSCAR BORG, 1906

Los Angeles Public Library

Autographs

Excerpt from remarks of Geo. C. Perkins in the United States Senate, May 12, 1896, advocating an appropriation for a deep-sea harbor at San Pedro, Los Angeles county.

"California has a coast as long as the distance from Maine to South Carolina--that is, California borders the Pacific for the same distance that the states between Maine and South Carolina border the Atlantic. In the southern part of California there has grown up the great metropolis of Los Angeles--the city of angels. It is located in the midst of one of the richest agricultural, horticultural, and viticultural sections of the country. It has vast and illimitable commercial possibilities; it has undeveloped mining resources; it is the central depot of two great transcontinental railroads, and is their terminus on the western side of this continent. The population of Los Angeles county has doubled every four years during the past two decades, and yet they come; and the people who come never go back except to visit their friends, for it is the paradise of this country. Its future I shall not attempt to describe, but it is as bright as the midday sun. x x x x

"When our government commenced work at Wilmington, Los Angeles county, in 1872 there was but 2 feet of water upon the bar at the entrance to that harbor; today there is 18 feet of water; and the appropriation proposed by the Committee on Commerce of $492,000 will give us, we believe, 22 feet of water. The harbor of Wilmington is capable of being enlarged and in time it will be a great commercial seaport--a harbor where there will be machine shops, graving docks, and all the appliances which are so necessary to foster and encourage a successful commerce. x x "

Yours Truly Geo. C. Perkins

GEORGE C. PERKINS, early 1900s

Los Angeles Public Library

Autographs

Mas Arai didn't believe in Jesus or Buddha, but thought there might be something in BACHI. In Japanese, BACHI was when you snapped at your wife, and then tripped on a rock in the driveway. You didn't suffer your punishment in another lifetime, but within the same life, even within the next few minutes.

Naomi Hirahara 平原直美

July 12, 2019

NAOMI HIRAHARA, 2019 • Mas Arai didn't believe in Jesus or Buddha, but thought there might be something in BACHI. In Japanese BACHI was when you snapped at your wife, and then tripped on a rock in the driveway. You didn't suffer your punishment in another lifetime, but within the same life, even within the next few minutes.

INSTITUTION FOR THE CHINESE BLIND, Incorporated (U.S.A.)

SHANGHAI, CHINA

(Interdenominational)

156 FIFTH AVENUE, NEW YORK • CHELSEA 2-3430

AMERICAN COMMITTEE

Officers

Honorary President
HELEN KELLER, LL.D.

President
ORRIN G. JUDD

Vice-President
BISHOP HERBERT WELCH, LL.D.

Secretary
EDGAR H. RUE

Treasurer
MORRIS W. EHNES

Advisory Committee

HOMER J. BUCKLEY
W. W. COMFORT, LL.D.
J. W. DECKER, D.D.
RALPH E. DIFFENDORFER, D.D.
C. K. EDMUNDS, Ph.D.
GEORGE A. FITCH, F.R.G.S.
MABEL C. GAGE
FRANK D. GAMEWELL, LL.D.
BISHOP IVAN LEE HOLT, LL.D.
ROBERT B. IRWIN, M.A.
ORRIN G. JUDD
HELEN KELLER, LL.D.
REV. JAMES A. MITCHELL
PAUL MONROE, LL.D.
NATHANIEL PEFFER
MARY PICKFORD
PAUL E. SCHERER, LL.D.
ROBERT E. SPEER, LL.D.
AMBASSADOR HU SHIH, LL.D.
BISHOP HERBERT WELCH, LL.D.
ANNA MAY WONG
CONSUL GENERAL
TSUNE-CHI YU, Ph.D.

February 10, 1941.

Dear Miss Haas:

Will you incline your ear to the war-harrassed blind in China who have climbed out of the depths to knowledge and friendship?

Once they were without education or hope. They were doubly shackled by the belief still prevalent in the Orient that the sightless are objects of divine wrath, and must endure their misfortune with passive fortitude. Neglect, scorn, grudging alms were all they could expect from society.

Then came Dr. Fryer with a redemptive faith to lift up their manhood and womanhood. Because of his noble work, they found life good for a while and dwelt in the House of the Lord with gladness.

Now a more cruel deprivation has overtaken them. Their beloved country is fighting for its very life, and they may not even vent their fervent patriotism by grasping a weapon in its defense. The school at Shanghai -- their brightest lamp -- has been broken. War's barbarism has wrecked the workshop -- their only means of economic self-help. Desperately they are trying to reoccupy the school that they may learn more. Unless they can take up their work again, they will sink in the cataclysm, and the hope of other blind people in China will be quenched.

Surely you will not let these reclaimed blind lose their light -- purpose, their shield and buckler -- the feeling that they may contribute their strength to the healing and rebuilding of their tortured fatherland. You who see -- you who live in peace -- you whose families are safe -- how can you help giving to the starving, menaced blind sons and daughters of as heroic a people as ever bled for freedom! Like Christian love, blindness knows no national frontier. It engirdles the world with Compassion of Him who bestowed His special care upon the exiles of the dark. Give then, - measure your donation by gratitude for the untold blessings you enjoy, and you will experience a sweetness in life that was not there before.

Hopefully and sincerely yours,

Helen Keller.

HELEN KELLER, 1941 • Letter sent to the Los Angeles Public Library

CHRIS KIEFER, 2018

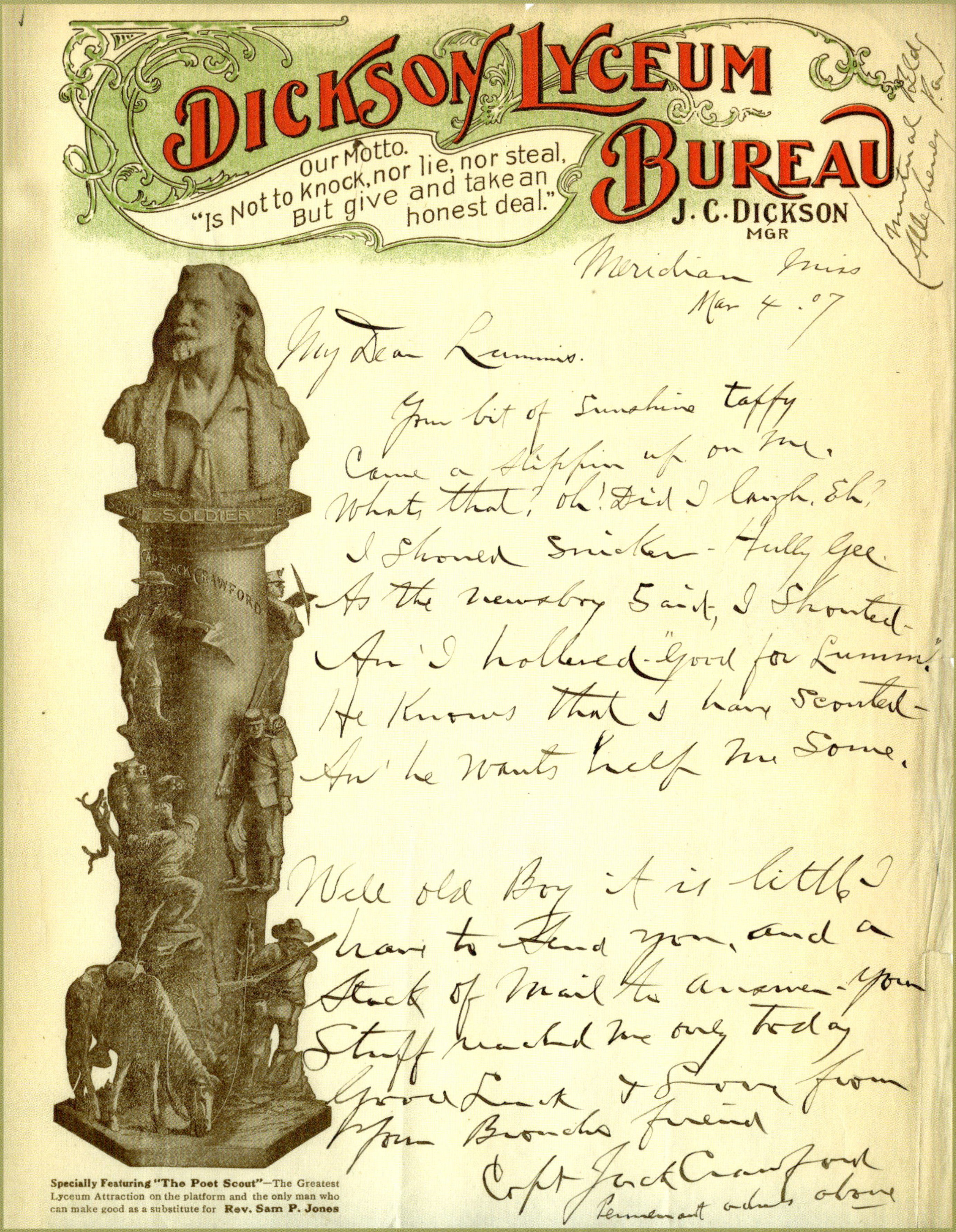

DICKSON LYCEUM BUREAU

Our Motto. "Is Not to knock, nor lie, nor steal, But give and take an honest deal."

J. C. DICKSON MGR

Specially Featuring "The Poet Scout"—The Greatest Lyceum Attraction on the platform and the only man who can make good as a substitute for Rev. Sam P. Jones

Meridian Miss
Mar 4 '07

My Dear Lummis.

Your bit of sunshine taffy
Came a slippin up on me.
What's that? Oh! Did I laugh, Eh?
I should snicker—Hully Gee.
As the newsboy said, I shouted—
An' I hollered—"Good for Lummis"
He Knows that I have scouted—
An' he wants help me some.

Well old Boy it is little I
have to send you, and a
stack of mail to answer—Your
Stuff reached me only today
Good Luck & Love from
Your Broncho friend

Capt Jack Crawford

Permanent address above

JOHN WALLACE CRAWFORD, "CAPTAIN JACK," 1907 • My Dear Lummis, Your bit of sunshine taffy Came a slippin up on me, What's that? Oh! Did I laugh, Eh? I should snicker. Hully Gee. As the newsboy I ain't, I shouted. An' I hollered —"Good for Lumm" He Knows that I have scouted An' he wants help me some. Well old Boy it is little I have to send you, and a stack of mail to answer. Your stuff reached me only today. Good luck and love from your Broncho friend

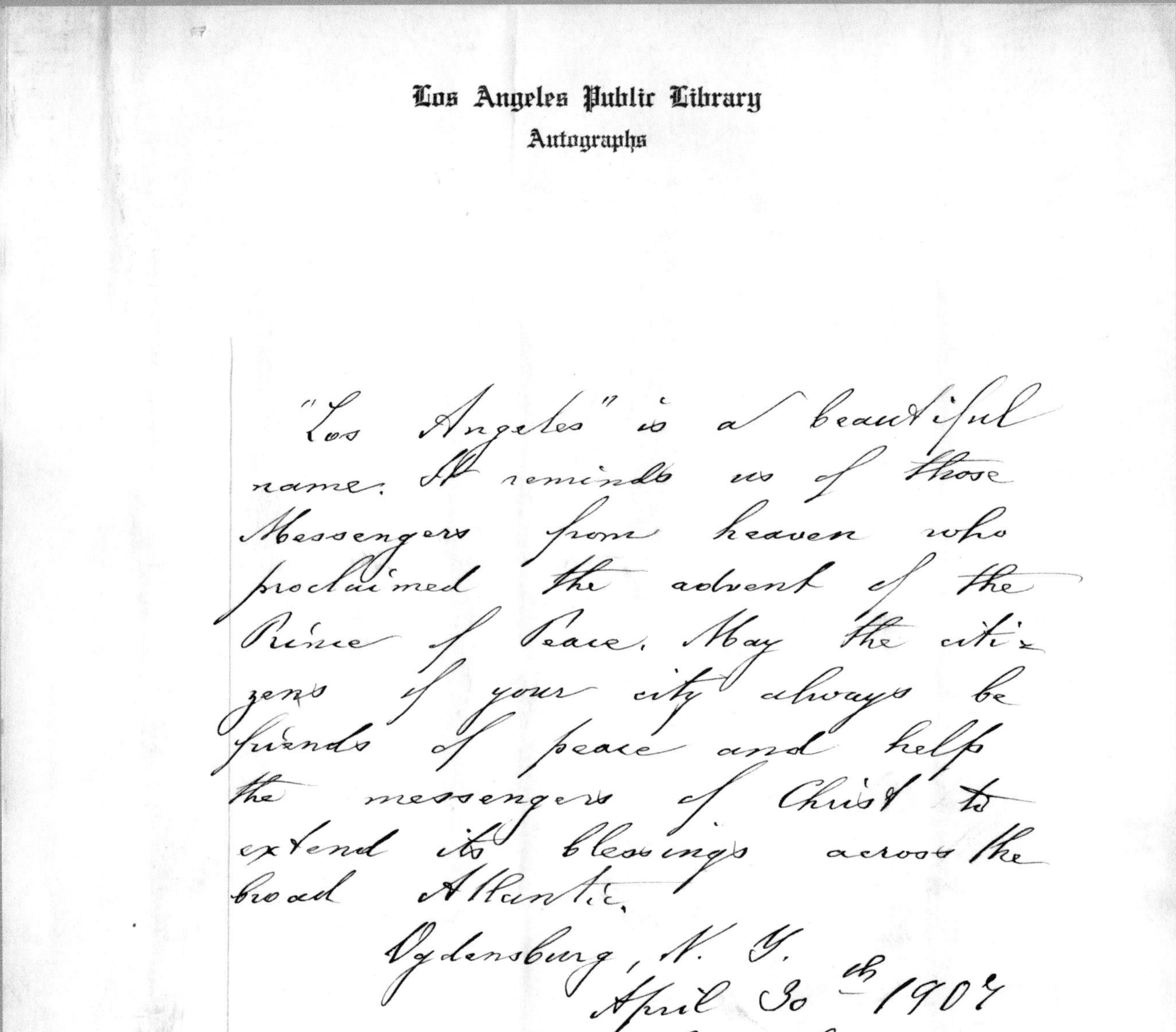

Los Angeles Public Library

Autographs

"Los Angeles" is a beautiful name. It reminds us of those Messengers from heaven who proclaimed the advent of the Prince of Peace. May the citizens of your city always be friends of peace and help the messengers of Christ to extend its blessings across the broad Atlantic.

Ogdensburg, N. Y.
April 30th 1907

+ H. Gabriels
Bishop of Ogdensburg.

HENRY GABRIELS, BISHOP OF OGDENSBURG, 1907 • "Los Angeles" is a beautiful name. It reminds us of those Messengers from heaven who proclaimed the advent of the Prince of Peace. May the citizens of your city always be friends of peace and help the messengers of Christ to extend its blessings across the broad Atlantic.

ADAM & TINA PRINCENTHAL, 2018

Los Angeles Public Library
Autographs

City Librarian
L. A. Calif.

Dear Friend Lummis:
I gladly comply with your autograph request for the Los Angeles Public Library and lose no time in affixing it here; dedicating the above squib to this institution and wishing it all success in the good it stands for and does.

Very sincerely
Joseph J. Mora...

Ocean Park. Calif.
Jan 31/07.

JOSEPH J. MORA, 1907 • Dear Friend Lummis, I gladly comply with your autograph request for The Los Angeles Public Library and lose no time in offering it here; dedicating the above squib to this institution and wishing it all success in the good it stands for and does.

Los Angeles Public Library
Autographs

Papi
Broken Bread
Kogi Por Vida
Locol 4 Life

ROY CHOI, 2019 • Papi, Broken Bread, Kogi *Por Vida*, Locol 4 Life

FAIRFAX BRANCH LIBRARY, 2018

EMILIE STEARNS PERRY, early 1900s

Los Angeles Public Library

Autographs

William Gillette
1908

Nothing to say.

WILLIAM GILLETTE, 1908 • Nothing to say.

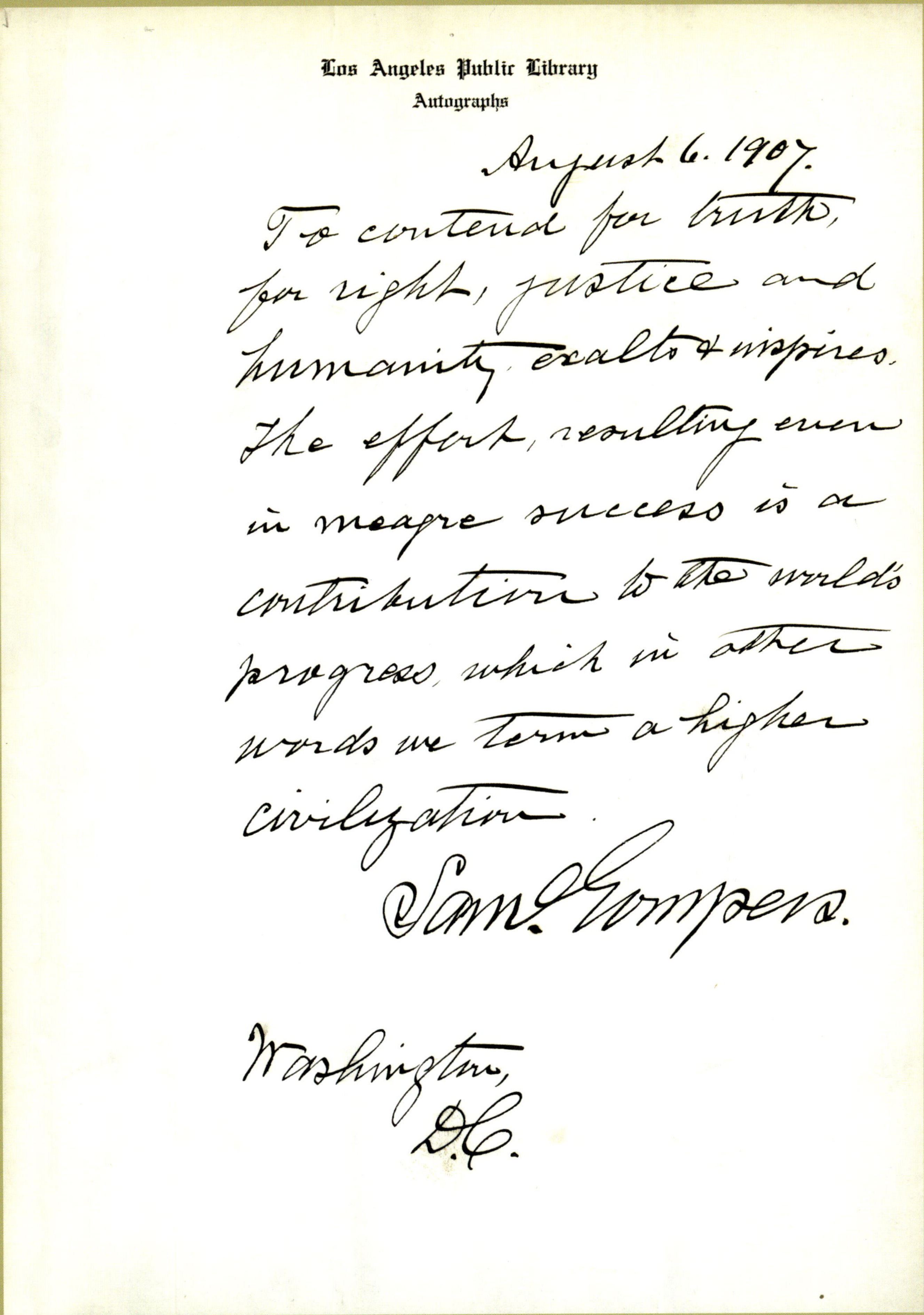

Los Angeles Public Library
Autographs

August 6. 1907.

To contend for truth, for right, justice and humanity, exalts & inspires. The effort, resulting even in meagre success is a contribution to the world's progress, which in other words we term a higher civilization.

Saml. Gompers.

Washington, D.C.

SAMUEL GOMPERS, 1907 • To contend for truth, for right, justice and humanity exalts and inspires. The effort, resulting even in meagre success is a contribution to the world's progress, which in other words we term a higher civilization.

Los Angeles Public Library
Autographs

The Desert: illimitable. majestic, reticent; immutable. yet ever changing: Opalescent, glowing with colour, yet tantalizing: elusive; fascinating to all who come but once beneath its strange allurement.

Hobart Bosworth.

Tempe Ariz.
1906.

HOBART BOSWORTH, 1906 • **The Desert: illimitable. Majestic, reticent; immutable. Yet ever changing: Opalescent, glowing with colour, yet tantalizing: elusive; fascinating to all who come but once beneath its strange allurement.**

Los Angeles Public Library

Autographs

The Stitchin' Sistahz Quilt Circle was formed in January 2013. It is a circle within the AAQLA (African American Quilters of. L.A.)

Our mission is to increase and share our quilting skills among each other and donate quilts to those undergoing chemotherapy and or dialysis.

Members

Linda Brooks
Ernestine Hadley
Barbara Johnson
Gwendolyn Jones
Mahasin Shamsiddeen
Elvis Smith
Mae O. Smith
Narvell Smith

Honorary Members

Barbara Beshears
Melvia Jones

THE STITCHIN' SISTAHZ QUILT CIRCLE, 2018

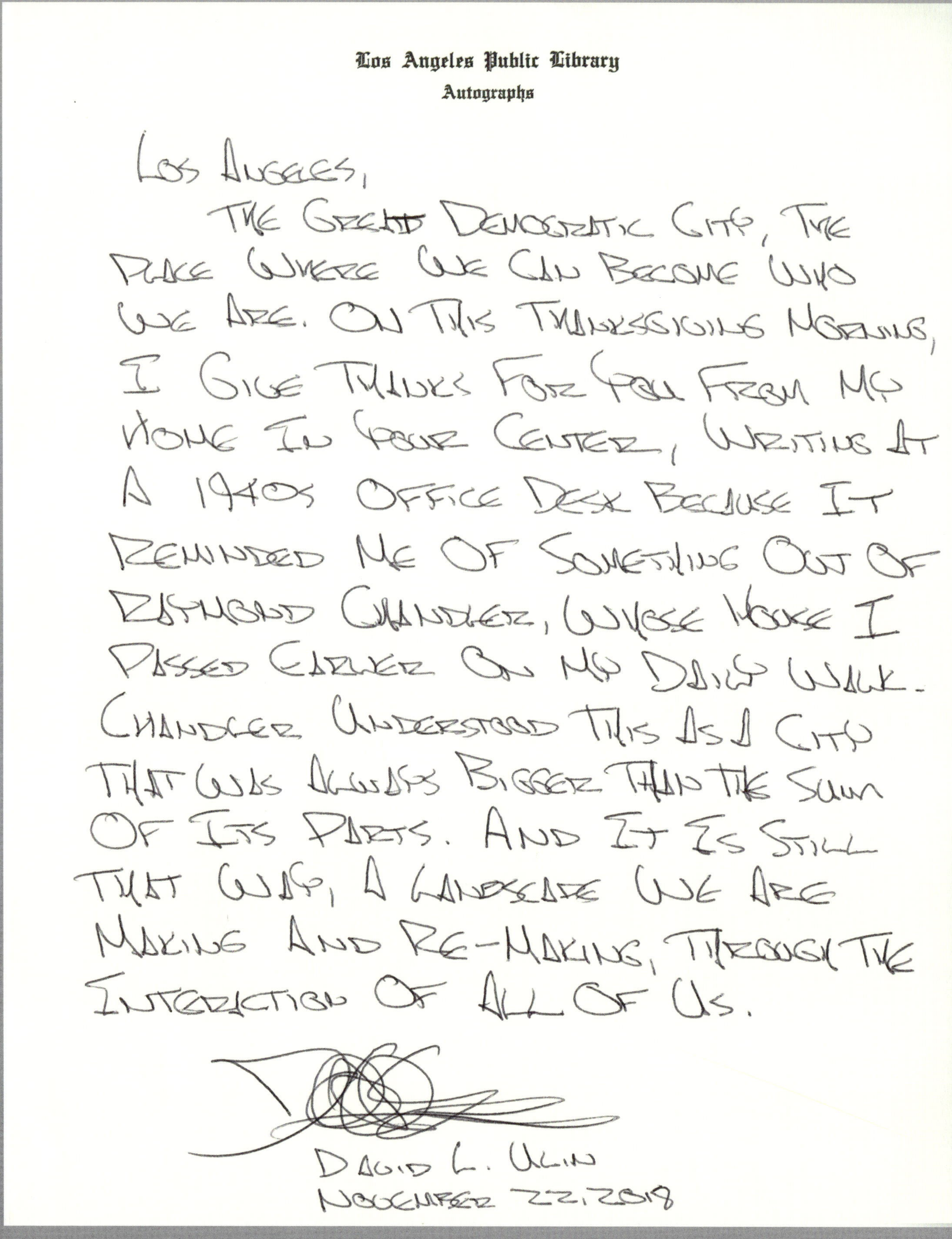

Los Angeles Public Library

Autographs

Los Angeles,

The Great Democratic City, The Place Where We Can Become Who We Are. On This Thanksgiving Morning, I Give Thanks For You From My Home In Your Center, Writing At A 1940s Office Desk Because It Reminded Me Of Something Out Of Raymond Chandler, Whose House I Passed Earlier On My Daily Walk. Chandler Understood This As A City That Was Always Bigger Than The Sum Of Its Parts. And It Is Still That Way, A Landscape We Are Making And Re-Making, Through The Interaction Of All Of Us.

David L. Ulin
November 22, 2018

DAVID L. ULIN, 2018 • Los Angeles, The great democratic city, the place where we can become who we are. On this Thanksgiving morning I give thanks for you from my home in your center, writing at a 1940s office desk because it reminded me of something out of Raymond Chandler, whose house I passed earlier on my daily walk. Chandler understood this as a city that was always bigger than the sum of its parts. And it is still that way, a landscape we are making and re-making, through the interaction of all of us.

MATTHEW CASTELLANOS, 2018

Los Angeles Public Library

Autographs

6/8/18

Anna Nelson was here!

ANNA NELSON, 2018

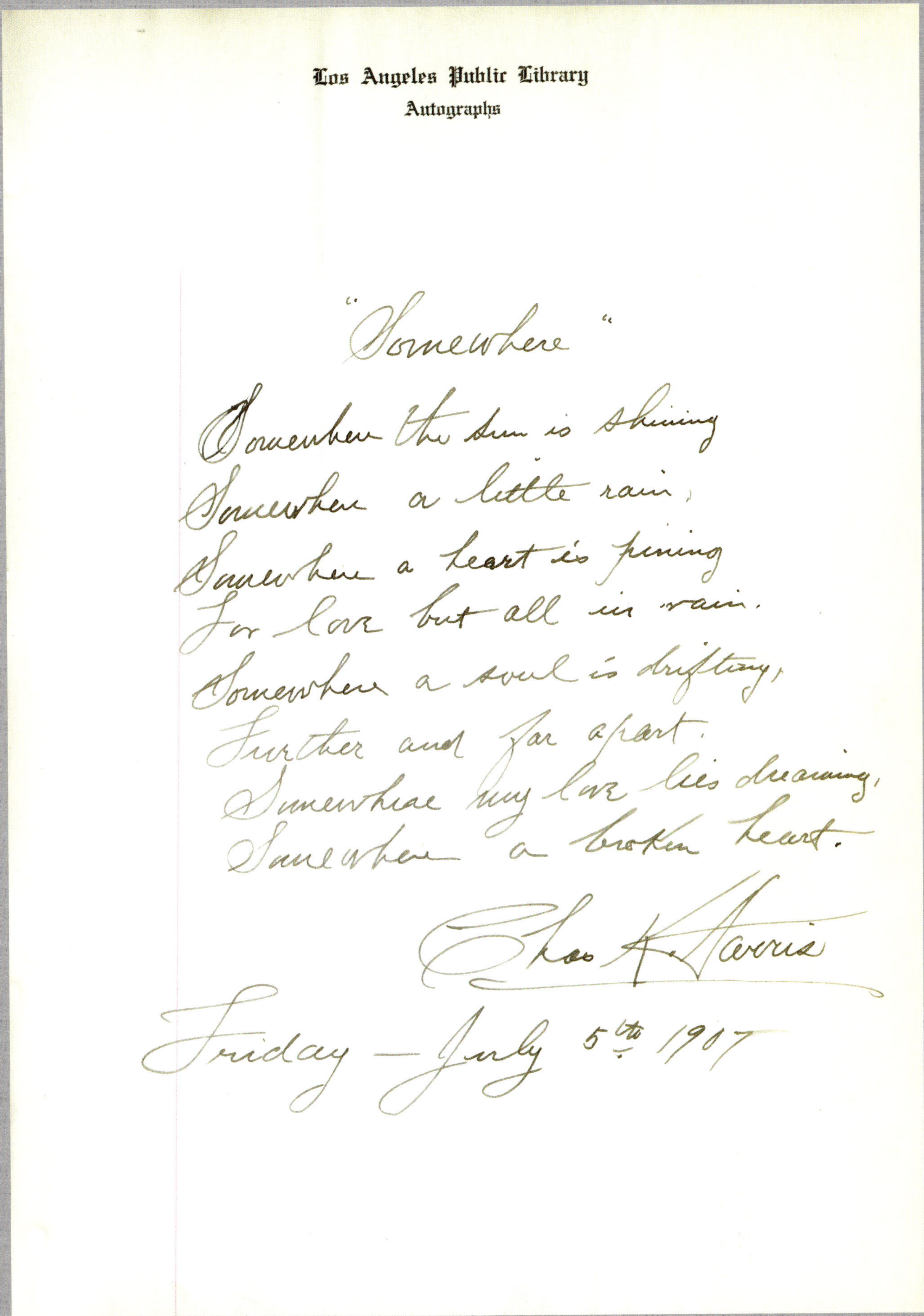

Los Angeles Public Library

Autographs

"Somewhere"

Somewhere the sun is shining

Somewhere a little rain,

Somewhere a heart is pining

For love but all in vain.

Somewhere a soul is drifting,

Further and far apart.

Somewhere my love lies dreaming,

Somewhere a broken heart.

Chas K. Harris

Friday — July 5th 1907

CHARLES K. HARRIS, 1907 • "Somewhere" Somewhere the sun is shining / Somewhere a little rain, / Somewhere a heart is pining, / For love but all in vain. / Somewhere a soul is drifting, / Further and far apart. / Somewhere my love lies dreaming, / Somewhere a broken heart.

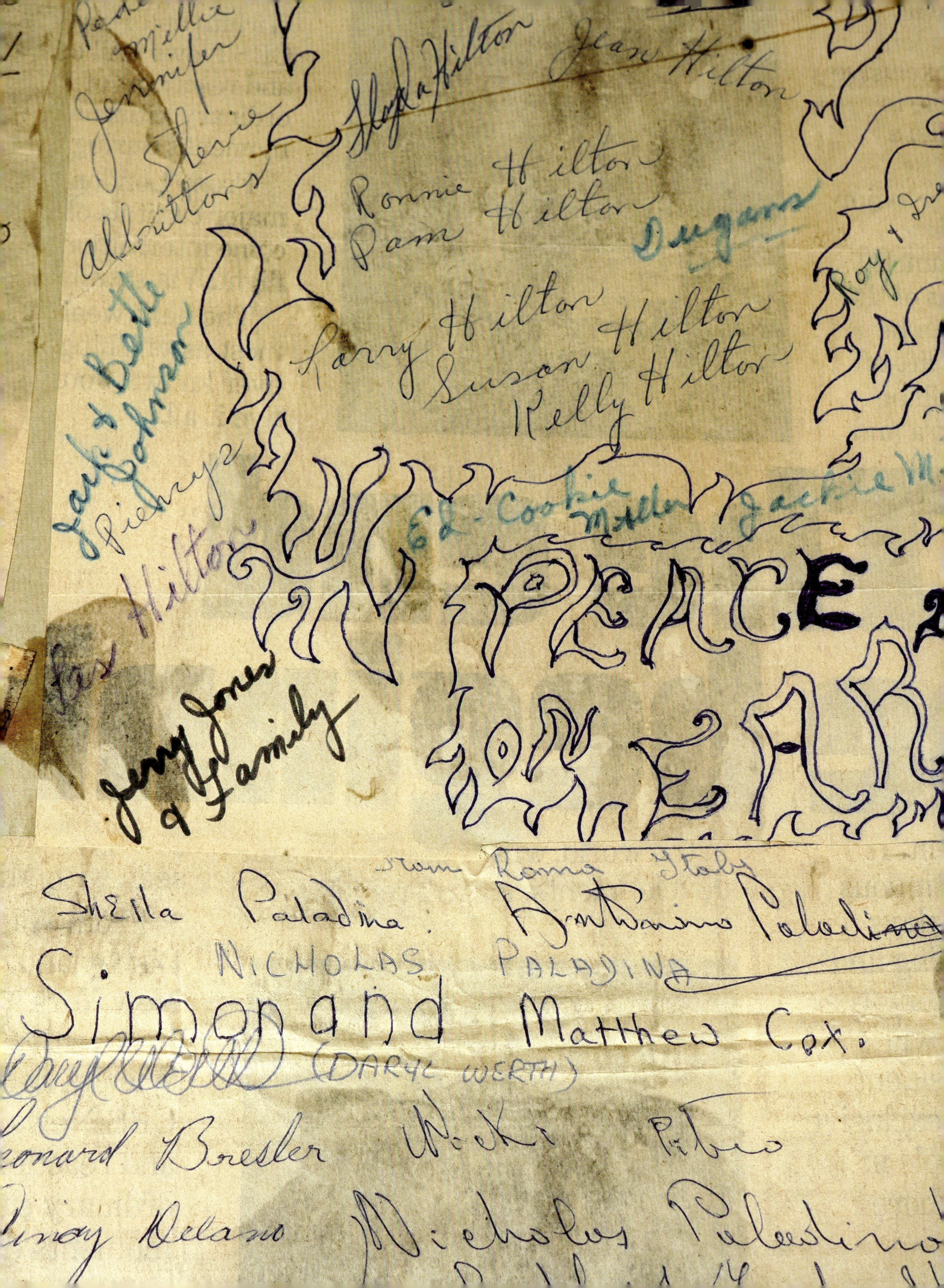

Jennifer
Stevie
Albrittons
Shayla Hilton
Jean Hilton
Ronnie Hilton
Pam Hilton
Dugans
Larry Hilton
Susan Hilton
Kelly Hilton
Jack & Bette Johnson
Ed - Cookie Miller
PEACE
ON EAR
Jerry Jones & Family
from Roma Italy
Sheila Paladina
NICHOLAS PALADINA
Simon and Matthew Cox.
(DARYL WERTH)
Breslor
Delano
Nicholas

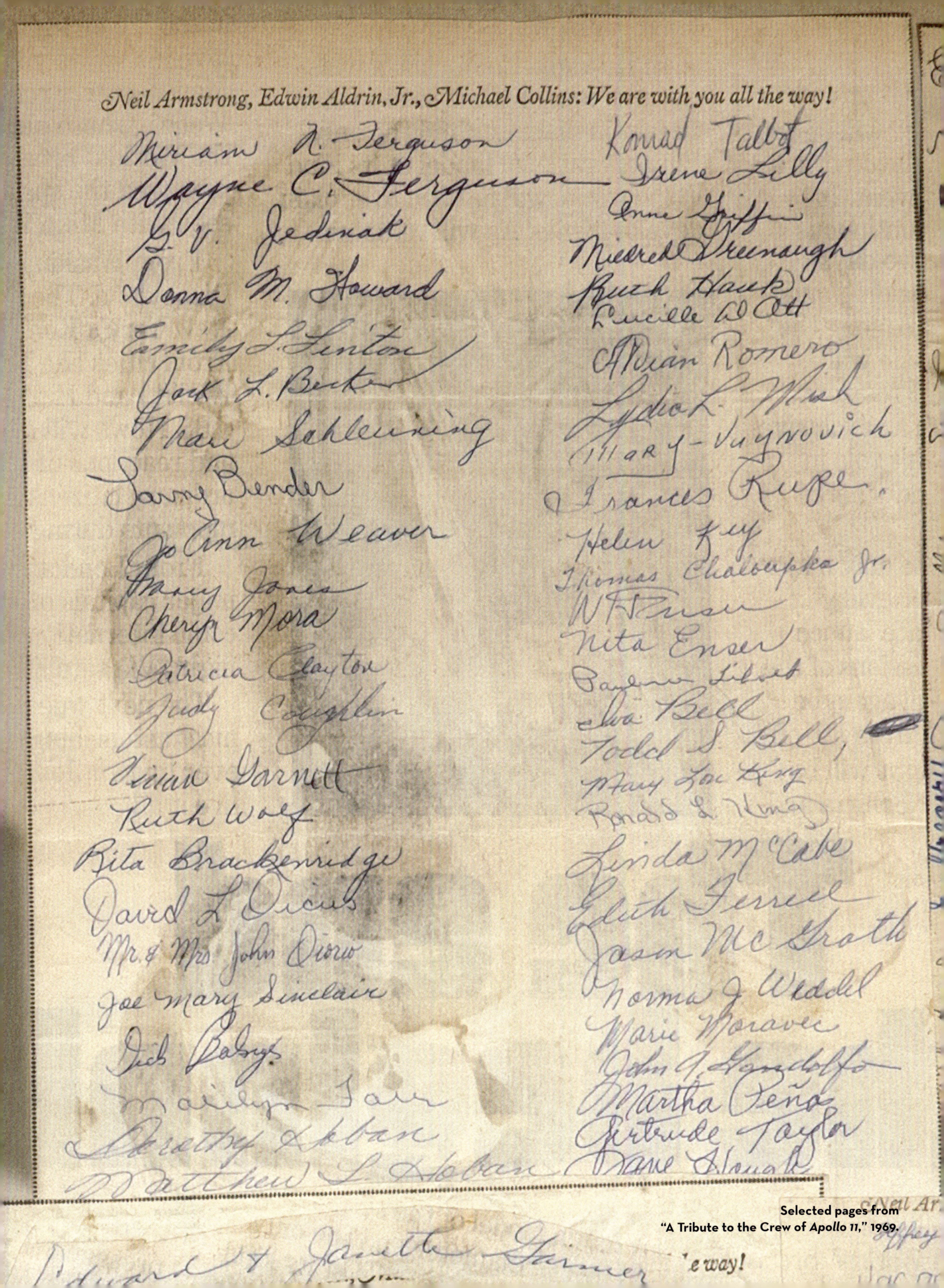

Neil Armstrong, Edwin Aldrin, Jr., Michael Collins: We are with you all the way!

Miriam R. Ferguson
Wayne C. Ferguson
G. V. Jedinak
Donna M. Howard
Emily S. Linton
Jack L. Becker
Marie Schleuning
Larry Bender
Jo Ann Weaver
Mary Jones
Cheryl Mora
Patricia Clayton
Judy Coughlin
Vivian Garnett
Ruth Wolf
Rita Brackenridge
David L. Dicus
Mr. & Mrs. John Diorio
Joe Mary Sinclair
Dick Babys
Marilyn Farr
Dorothy Hoban
Matthew L. Hoban

Konrad Talbot
Irene Lilly
Anne Griffin
Mildred Greenhaugh
Ruth Hauk
Lucille D. Ott
Adrian Romero
Lydia L. Mish
Mary Vuynovich
Frances Ruge
Helen Key
Thomas Chaloupka Jr.
W. H. Enser
Nita Enser
Bayerna Libert
Iva Bell
Todd S. Bell
Mary Lou King
Ronald L. King
Linda McCabe
Edith Ferrell
Jason McGrath
Norma J. Weddel
Marie Moravec
John J. Gandolfo
Martha Peña
Gertrude Taylor
Diane Hough

Edward & Janette Grimer

Selected pages from "A Tribute to the Crew of *Apollo 11*," 1969.

FERNANDO VALENZUELA

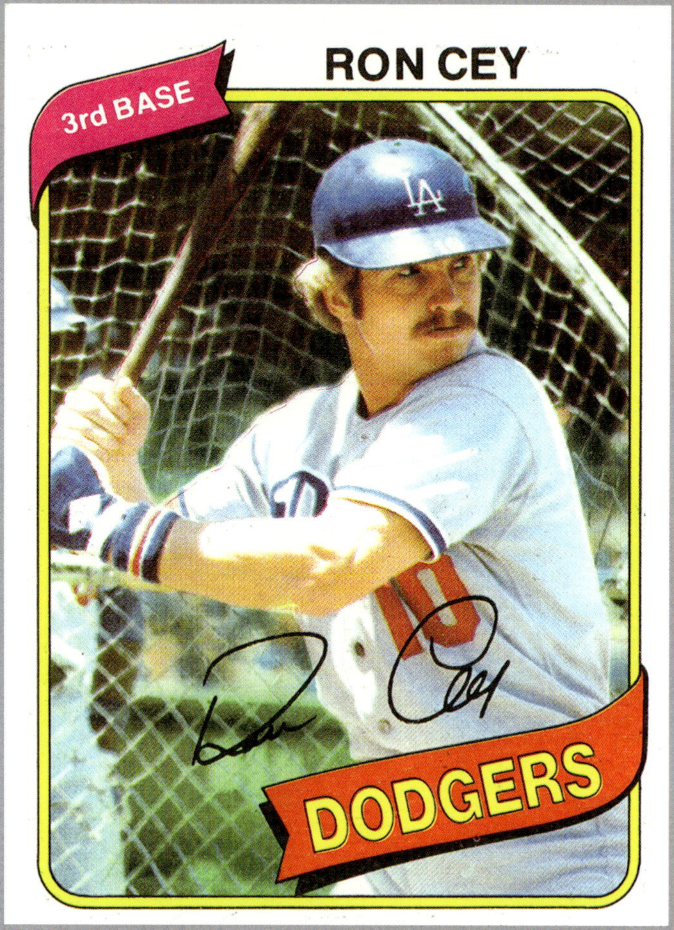

RON CEY

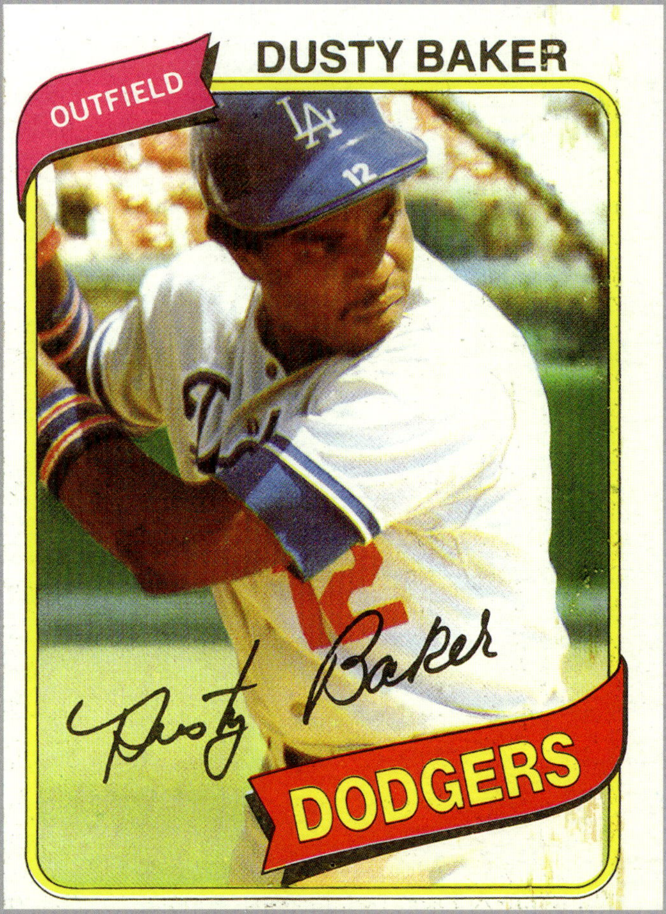

DUSTY BAKER

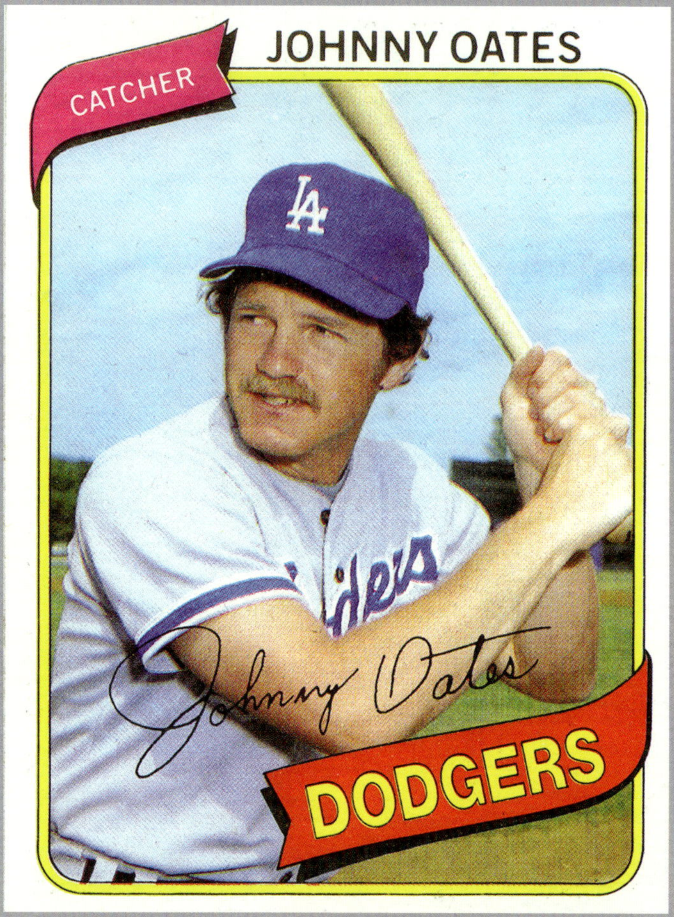

JOHNNY OATES

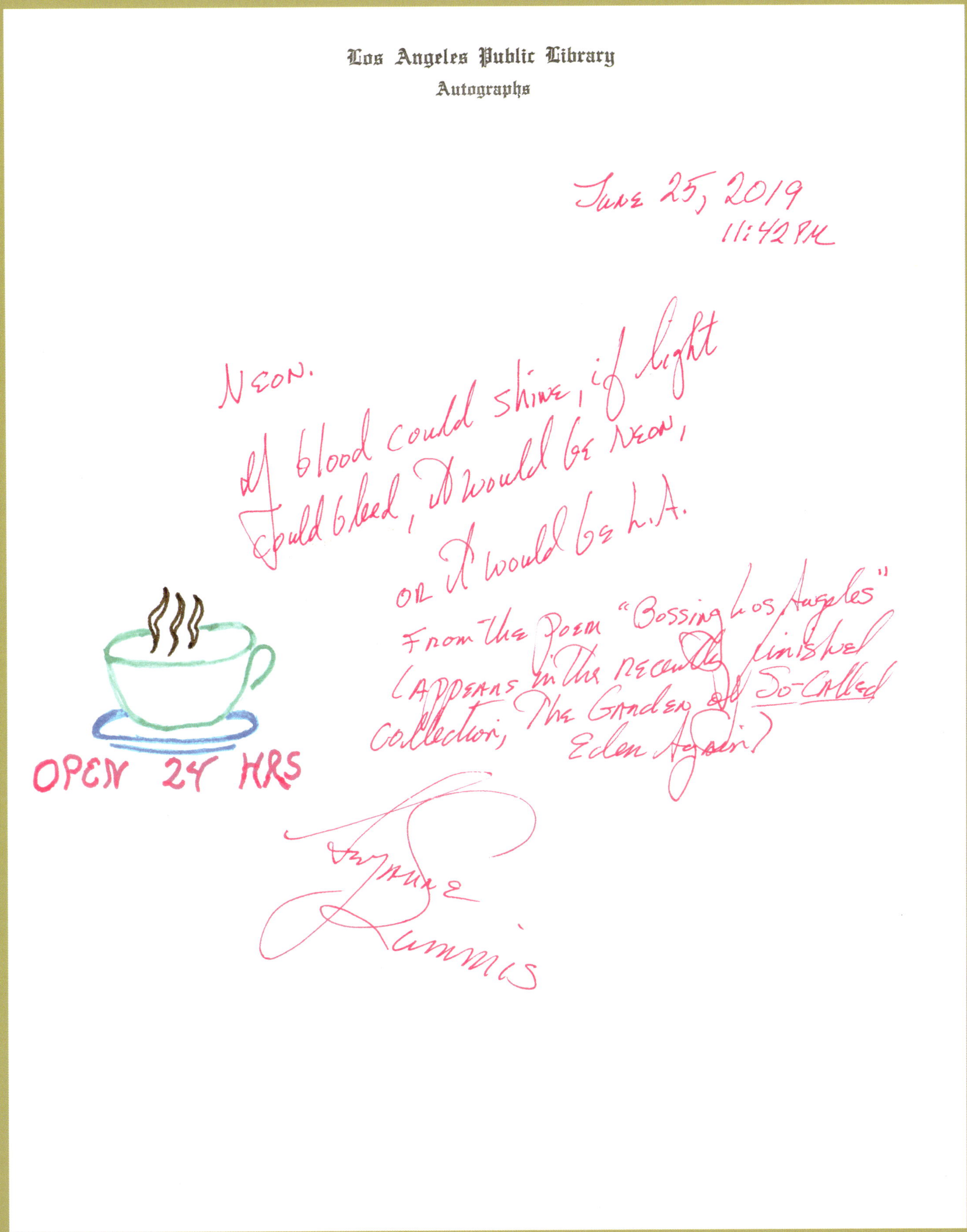

Los Angeles Public Library

Autographs

June 25, 2019
11:42 PM

Neon.

If blood could shine, if light
could bleed, it would be neon,
or it would be L.A.

From the poem "Bossing Los Angeles"
(Appears in the recently finished
collection, The Garden of So-Called
Eden Again)

Suzanne
Lummis

SUZANNE LUMMIS, 2019 • "Neon" If blood could shine, if light could bleed, it would be neon, or it would be L.A. From the poem "Bossing Los Angeles" (Appears in the recently finished collection, *The Garden of So-Called Eden Again*)

Los Angeles Public Library

Autographs

To the
Librarians,
who saved
millions from
despair.
[illegible signature]

JOHN RECHY, 2019 • To the Librarians, who saved millions from despair.

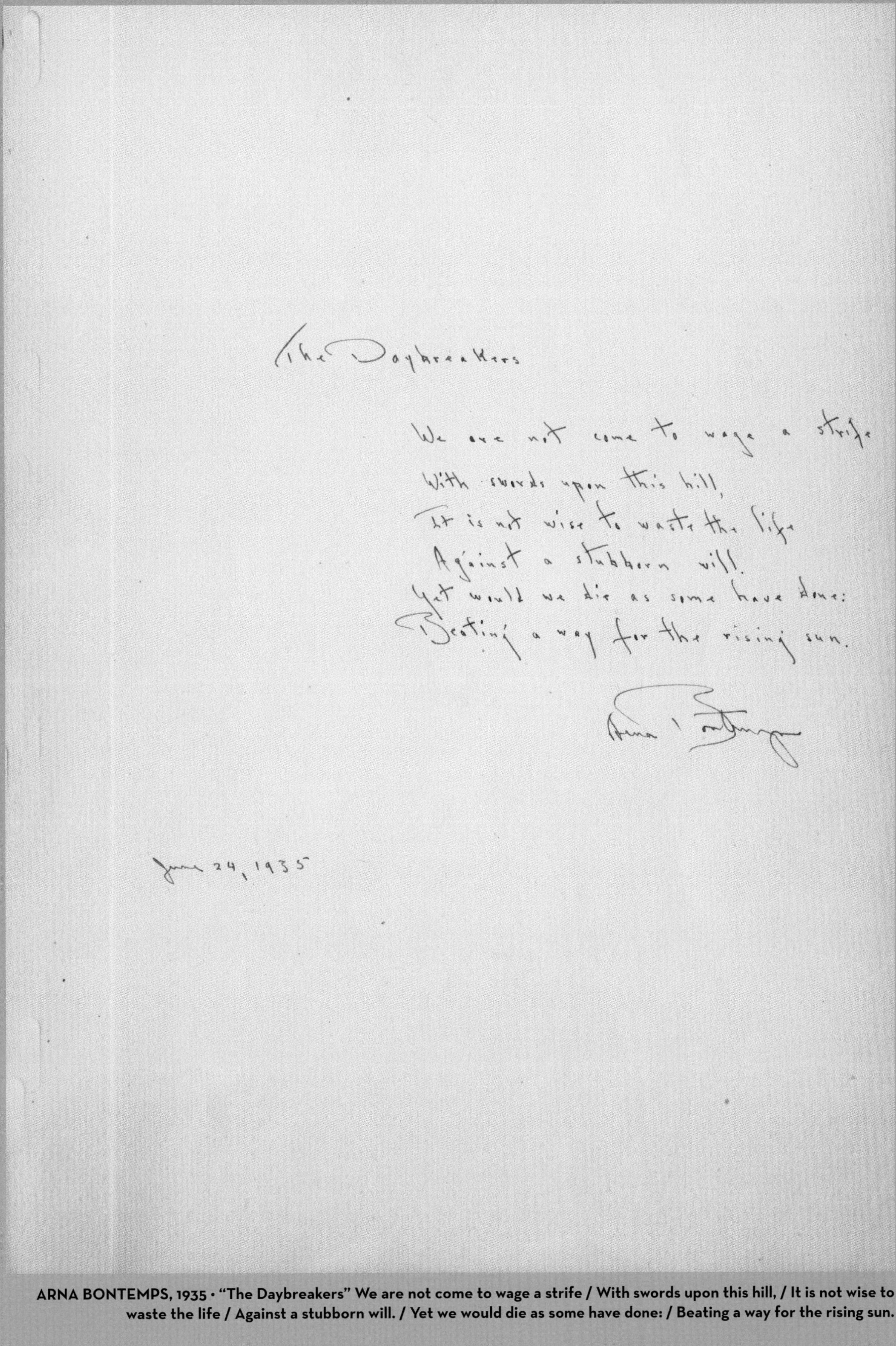

The Daybreakers

We are not come to wage a strife
With swords upon this hill,
It is not wise to waste the life
Against a stubborn will.
Yet would we die as some have done:
Beating a way for the rising sun.

Arna Bontemps

June 24, 1935

ARNA BONTEMPS, 1935 • **"The Daybreakers" We are not come to wage a strife / With swords upon this hill, / It is not wise to waste the life / Against a stubborn will. / Yet we would die as some have done: / Beating a way for the rising sun.**

Los Angeles Public Library

Autographs

How blind is he who, powerless
to discern
The glories that about his pathway
burn,
Walks unaware the avenues of
Dream,
Nor sees the domes of Paradise
agleam!
O Golden Age! to him more no-
bly planned
Thy light lies ever upon sea
and land.
From sordid scenes he lifts
his soul at will,
And sees a Grecian god on
every hill!

Ambrose Bierce.

Washington, D.C.,
February 8, 1907.

AMBROSE BIERCE, 1907 • How blind is he who, powerless to discern / The glories that about his pathway burn, / Walks unaware the avenues of Dream, / Nor sees the domes of Paradise agleam! / O Golden Age, to him more nobly planned / Thy light lies ever upon sea and land. / From sordid scenes he lifts his soul at will / And sees a Grecian god on every hill!

Los Angeles Public Library
Autographs

Tongva women
have never left their land
they just became
invisible

To be visable

Julia L. Bogany

JULIA L. BOGANY, 2019

Los Angeles Public Library
Autographs

ESTEVAN ORIOL, 2018

Los Angeles Public Library

Autographs

Equality of the Sexes.

On all the broad lines of humanity women and men are alike. Alike they suffer from hunger and cold, alike they enjoy comfort and luxury. Alike they are uplifted by prosperity and cast down by adversity, hand in hand they walk through life, side by side they slumber in the grave.

It cannot even be said that intellect belongs to man alone, for there are some brilliant women, and, it must be admitted, there are some stupid men.

Seeing then that they are thus alike, thus closely associated, sister and brother, husband and wife, should they not have an equal voice in government and be equal sharers in the birth-right of liberty—

Lillie Devereux Blake

President New York Legislative League

April 19. 1907

LILLIE DEVEREUX BLAKE, 1907 • Equality of the Sexes: On all the broad lines of humanity women and men are alike. Alike they suffer from hunger and cold, alike they enjoy comfort and luxury. Alike they are uplifted by prosperity and cast down by adversity, hand in hand they walk through life, side by side they slumber in the grave. It can never be said that intellect belongs to man alone, for there are some brilliant women and, it must be admitted, there are some stupid men. Seeing then that they are thus alike, thus closely associated, sister and brother, husband and wife, should they not have an equal voice in government and be equal sharers in the birthright of liberty.

PETER SHIRE, 2019

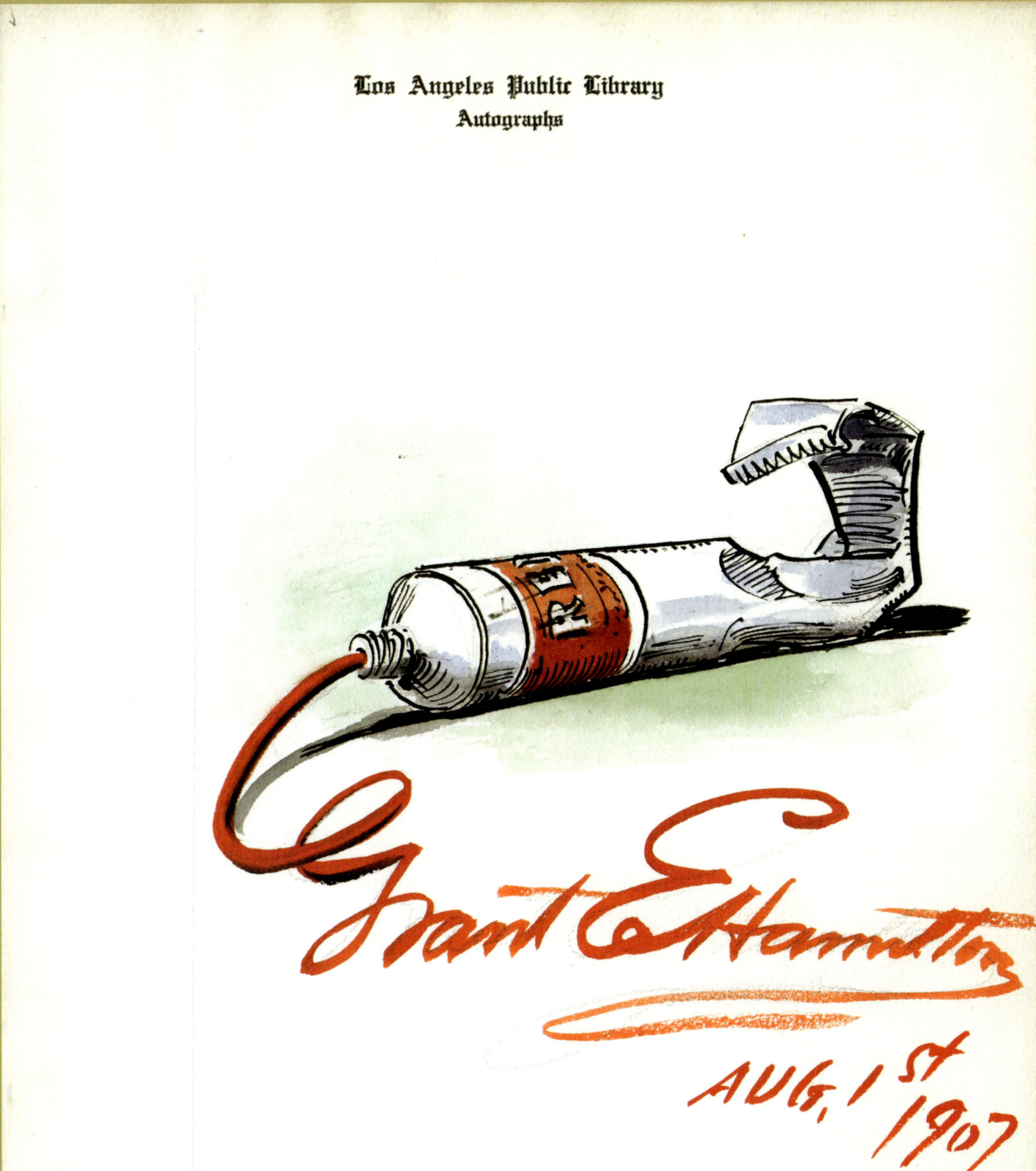

GRANT E. HAMILTON, 1907

Sarita Montiel autographs a picture for fans at Gonzalez Restaurant, circa 1950.

ENDNOTES

- Page 37: **"Broad avenues, lined with Chinese pictographs**. . . Hector Tobar, *The Tattooed Soldier* (Penguin, 1998), 3.
- Page 39: **In 1892, after a visit to the Grand Canyon. . .** Charles Lummis, *Some Strange Corners of Our Country: The Wonderland of the Southwest* (The Century Co., 1892), 163.
- Page 39: **Centuries earlier, Spanish explorers and colonists**. . . Ibid., 167.
- Page 39: **Of course, signatures he cherished**. . . Campbell Grant, *The Rock Art of the North American Indians* (Cambridge UP, 1983), 7.
- Page 41: **His anti-Indian sentiment was more subdued the second time around**. . . Charles Lummis, "The Autograph Cliff, El Morro," *Land of Sunshine* (Land of Sunshine Publishing Co, 1896), 101.
- Page 41: **Seven years before his first visit to El Morro. . .** Mark Thompson, *American Character: The Curious Life of Charles Fletcher Lummis and the Rediscovery of the Southwest* (Arcade, 2001), 1.
- Page 41: **Lummis first honed his self-branding skills as a college student**. . . Ibid., 13.
- Page 41: **As Kevin Starr described it, El Alisal**. . . Daniel P. Moneta and Patricia A. Butz, "Lummis in California Life," in Moneta (ed) *Charles Fletcher Lummis: The Centennial Exhibition* (Southwest Museum, 1985), 49.
- Page 43: **Lummis had a kindred contemporary spirit in Austrian writer Stefan Zweig**. . . Christine Nelson, "Of Love and Magic," in Nelson (ed) *The Magic of Handwriting: The Pedro Correa do Lago Collection, The Morgan Library and Museum* (Taschen, 2018), 23.
- Page 43: **"Librarian Lummis sheds corduroy; keeps old hat,". . .** Thompson, *American Character*, 272
- Page 43: **There was nothing stiff collar about Lummis's five year term as City Librarian**. . . Ibid., 280–282; Turbesé Lummis Fiske and Keith Lummis, *Charles F. Lummis: The Man and His West* (University of Oklahoma Press, 1975); Susan Orlean also recently summarized these previous accounts of Lummis's time as city librarian in *The Library Book* (Simon & Schuster, 2018), 138–155.
- Page 43: **He wanted the library to be a "university of the people"**. . . Orlean, *The Library Book*, 146–147.
- Page 45: **The idea first hit him in 1905**. . . Charles Lummis, Report to the Board of the L.A. Public Library, October, 1905. Collections of the Los Angeles Public Library.
- Page 45: **Lummis's plan was not to just create the archive**. . . "Autograph Exhibit." *Los Angeles Times* (1886–1922), December 19, 1909, Proquest Historical Newspapers: *Los Angeles Times*, p. I12; "Public Library Autographs." *Los Angeles Times* (1886–1922), January 27, 1910, ProQuest Historical Newspapers: *Los Angeles Times*. p. II14; "World Celebrities' Autographs Collected By The Los Angeles Public Library." *Los Angeles Times* (1886–1922), November 28, 1909, Proquest Historical Newspapers: *Los Angeles Times*. p. Ii14.
- Page 45: **L.A. was still a city in search of itself, a "half-horse town"**. . . David Ulin, *Sidewalking: Coming to Terms with Los Angeles* (UC Press, 2015), 33.
- Page 45: **Just who constituted the "social polity" of L.A. was up for grabs**. . . Kevin Starr, *Americans and the California Dream 1850–1915* (Oxford University Press, 1973), 397–401, 414, 441.
- Page 47: **By the nineteenth century, autograph collecting in the U.S. was all the rage as a popular hobby**. . . Jessica Helfand, *Scrapbooks: An American History* (Yale University Press, 2008) xvii. See also Nathaniel Adams, "The Lives of the Autograph Collectors" (https://rarebookschool.org/2005/exhibitions/autographs.shtml) and Raab Collection, "The Lure of Collecting Autographs" (https://www.raabcollection.com/learning/history-autograph-collecting)
- Page 47: **As early as 1815, William B. Sprague had emerged**. . . Tamara Plakins Thornton, *Handwriting in America: A Cultural History* (Yale University Press, 1996), 87.
- Page 47: **Autographs were "talismans of individuality,"**. . . Ibid., 85, 88.
- Page 47: **His 1841 essays for Graham's Magazine**. . . Edgar Allan Poe, *Edgar Allan Poe Analyzes Handwriting: A Chapter on Autography* (Jim Chevalier, 2004), 10.
- Page 47: **The first full-length study of handwriting analysis**. . . Thornton, *Handwriting in America: A Cultural History*, *74*. Also see Ann Trubek, *The History and Uncertain Future of Handwriting* (Bloomsbury, 2016), 98–110.
- Page 50: **More earnest in its efforts to create a democracy of signatures**. . . Originally intended as a welcome home gift to Neil Armstrong, Buzz Aldrin, and Michael Collins, the Apollo 11 autograph book is now part of the LAPL's Special Collections.
- Page 53: **By 1939, the culture of the autograph**. . . Lee Shippey and Max Yavno, *The Los Angeles Book* (Houghton Mifflin, 1950), 43.

- Page 55: **The rise of the autograph in the nineteenth century was linked**. . . Nathaniel Adams, "The Lives of the Autograph Collectors" (https://rarebookschool.org/2005/exhibitions/autographs.shtml).
- Page 55: **The tradition flourished in the Renaissance**. . . See the Getty Research Institute project *LA Liber Amicorum* (http://www.getty.edu/research/special_collections/notable/la_liber_amicorum/index.html). Also Violet Snow, *"The Rise and Fall of the Autograph Book" (https://hudsonvalleyone.com/2017/12/28/the-rise-and-fall-of-the-autograph-book/)*
- Page 61: **The earliest known evidence of a human signature**. . . Vik Muniz, "Tangible Time," in *The Magic of Handwriting*, 13–14.
- Page 61: **In Phillips's many studies of L.A. . .** Susan A. Phillips, "Notes from the Margins: *Graffiti, Community, and Environment in Los Angeles," Journal of the West*, Spring 2009, Vol. 48, No. 2; Susan A. Phillips, *Wallbangin: Graffiti and Gangs in L.A.* (University of Chicago Press, 1999); Susan A. Phillips, *The City Beneath: A Century of Los Angeles Graffiti* (Yale University Press, 2019)
- Page 61: **The total result is a boundless urban inventory of names**. . . Doreen Massey, *For Space* (Sage, 2005).
- Page 63: **The autograph's fight against mortality**. . . Susan Brind Morrow, *The Names of Things: A Passage in the Egyptian Desert* (Riverhead, 1997), 4.
- Page 63: **The city is full of autograph books carved in concrete**. . . Susan A. Phillips, *Wallbangin: Graffiti and Gangs in L.A.* (University of Chicago Press, 1999); Steve Grody, *Graffiti L.A.: Street Styles and Art* (Abrams, 2007); Stefano Bloch, "Why Do Graffiti Writers Write on Murals? The Birth, Life, and Slow Death of Freeway Murals in Los Angeles," in International Journal of Urban and Regional Research, 2016.
- Page 63: **And in this "thirty-five-miles-per-hour" city**. . . Ulin, *Sidewalking*, 2.
- Page 63: **When "the places associated with people who have limited power are more likely to be destroyed,"**. . . Laura Pulido, Laura Barraclough, and Wendy Cheng, *A People's Guide to Los Angeles* (UC Press, 2012), 10.
- Page 63: **Whose names should be on the wall, on the street name, on the freeway sign**. . . Erin Schneider, "Interchange: Los Angeles and its Freeways," https://www.are.na/erin-schneider/la-freeway-memorials; Sharon Mizota, "Community's the Thing: Susan Silton Examines the Power of Names," May 2013 https://www.kcet.org/shows/artbound/communitys-the-thing-susan-silton-examines-the-power-of-names; Bloch, "Why Do Graffiti Writers Write on Murals?"
- Page 63: **Whose city is it**. . . Henri Lefebvre, *Le Droit a la ville* (Paris : Anthropos, 1968). David Harvey, "The Right to the City," *New Left Review* 53 2008.
- Page 65: **Like so many other abandoned structures in the city's history**. . . David L. Ulin, "City of Ruins: How Norman Klein Has Emerged as the City's Most Innovative Social Critic," *Los Angeles Magazine*, December 2004.
- Page 67: **The balloon "throwie"**. . . I thank Manuel Pastor for flagging this for me and Susan Phillips for helping in identifying the artists.
- Page 67: **Names written into sidewalks in the 1940s**. . . I thank Chaz Bojórquez for sharing this with me.
- Page 67: **There is no history of layering without the companion history**. . . Erin M. Curtis, Jessica Hough, and Guisela Latorre (eds), ¡Murales Rebeldes!: L.A. Chicana/Chicano Murals Under Siege (Angel City Press, 2017).
- Page 69: **Herrón and Gronk, as members of pioneering Chicano art collective Asco**. . . Chon Noriega, "Conceptual Graffiti and the Public Art Museum: Spray Paint LACMA," in C. Ondine Chavoya and Rita Gonzalez (eds) *Asco: Elite of the Obscure* (Hatje Cantz, 2011), 256.
- Page 69: **Whitewashing doesn't need paint**. . . Erin M. Curtis, "A Legal Legacy," in ¡Murales Rebeldes!: L.A. Chicana/Chicano Murals Under Siege (Angel City Press, 2017), 80–101.
- Page 69: **For historian William Deverell**. . . William Deverell, *Whitewashed Adobe: The Rise of Los Angeles and the Remaking of Its Mexican Past* (UC Press, 2004); Carey McWilliams, *Southern California: An Island on the Land* (Peregrine Smith, 1973).
- Page 69: **Similarly, Norman Klein has written of Los Angeles**. . . Norman M. Klein, *The History of Forgetting: Los Angeles and the Erasure of Memory* (Verso, 1997), 3.
- Page 71: **The glyphs and calligraphy of gangs**. . . Francois Chastanet, ed. *Cholo Writing: Latino Gang Graffiti in Los Angeles* (Dokument Press, 2009); Jerry Romotsky and Sally R. Romotsky, *Los Angeles Barrio Calligraphy* (Dawson's Book Shop, 1976); Susan A. Phillips, *Wallbangin: Graffiti and Gangs in L.A.* (University of Chicago Press, 1999).
- Page 73: **In 2018, all major U.S. credit card companies announced**. . . Stacy Cowley, "Credit card signatures are about to become extinct in the U.S.," *New York Times*, April 8, 2018.
- Page 79: **In her ongoing installation, Crenshaw District Hieroglyphics Project**. . . Mark Pieterson, "We Built This City: A Conversation with Lauren Halsey," *Art in America*, June 7, 2018.

ACKNOWLEDGMENTS

AS WITH ALL OF THE BOOKS in this series, *The Autograph Book of L.A.* would not be possible without the incredible support of Ken Brecher, the Library Foundation of Los Angeles, and City Librarian John F. Szabo; Paddy Calistro, Scott McAuley, and Terri Accomazzo of Angel City Press are a dream publishing crew; and Amy Inouye of Future Studio Design has given each of the books the visual identity that has made people pick them up.

For this project I benefited greatly from the research assistance, editorial work, and creative wisdom of USC Annenberg School of Communication doctoral student Franny Corry, who shaped the project with me from the start. Students in my 2017 USC class To Live and Die in Los Angeles, joined me in doing some of the initial biographical research on the Lummis collection. Todd Lerew of the Library Foundation of Los Angeles was a constant source of support, suggestions, and research assistance. LAPL Senior Librarian Xochitl Oliva, Digitization & Special Collections, is the shepherd, champion, and guru of the Autograph Collection and was invaluable to me in understanding and accessing the collections and in preparing collection materials for this book. Librarian Rudy Ruiz at LAPL also played a pivotal early role in sourcing key documents, and the incredible photos featured would never have seen the light of day without the expert assistance of Senior Librarian of the Photo Collection Christina Rice. Liza Posas of the Autry Museum of the American West provided guidance and support for our use of Lummis's guest books. When it came to reproducing the original autograph stationery, the team at Aardvark Letterpress were the ideal partners. The 2018 Autograph Day would not have been possible without the work of Kian Daizadeh, Joyce Cooper, and all the dedicated librarians and staff at the nineteen participating branch libraries across the city.

Special thanks to Shepard Fairey and Chaz Bojórquez for taking the time to participate in the project and share their knowledge with me, and extra gratitude to Susan A. Phillips for being so generous with her knowledge and research, and for helping me solve a few last-minute mysteries.

As always, I couldn't have written this book without the patience and love of Ceci and Yamila, whose autographs I cherish above all others.

—J.K.

AUTOGRAPH INDEX

Jane Addams, 156
Elizabeth Akers, 182
Aisha Ali, 155
Rasmus Bjørn Anderson, 131
Angelyne, 40
Anonymous seafarer, 90-91
A-No.1, 88
Apollo 11, 110, 136-137, 178, 204-205
Marie Azpiroz, 158
Dusty Baker, 206
Kari Barba, 117
Mary A. Bartow, 150
Katharine Lee Bates, 20
L. Frank Baum, 119
James Carroll Beckwith, 168
Ambrose Bierce, 210
Lillie Devereux Blake, 213
Julia L. Bogany, 211
Chaz Bojórquez, 99, 100
Arna Bontemps, 209
Carl Oscar Borg, 184
Hobart Bosworth, 198
J. Boyle, 132
Charles Bukowski, 76
Carl Bulosan, 171
Elbridge Ayer Burbank, 68
Barbara Carrasco, 70
Matthew Castellanos, 201
Ron Cey, 206
Charline, 82-83
Charles Waddell Chesnutt, 164
Roy Choi, 193
Randall Cindrich, 151
Florence Earle Coates, 133
Alex Cohen, 157
Ina Coolbrith, 181
René Corado, 153
John Wallace Crawford, 138, 189
Xavier Cugat, 125
Cyrus Edwin Dallin, 127
John Cotton Dana, 180
Homer Davenport, 167
Eugene V. Debs, 172
Sandra de la Loza, 176
W.W. Denslow, 5
Richard Elwood Dodge, 16
Franky Dominguez, 166
Mercedes Dorame, 124
William Henry Drake, 44
Wendy Escobar, 130
Jesus Esparza, 173
Ireri Espinoza-Taboada, 146
Shepard Fairey, 25
Fairfax Branch Library, 194
Priscilla Fernandez, 102
Ron Finley, 114
Friends of Griffith Park, 143
Gajin Fujita, 30
Henry Gabriels, 190
Edmund Waller Gale, 135
Willie Garing "Willie G.", 86-87
Lynell George, 170
William Gillette, 196
Charlotte Perkins Gilman, 109
Samuel Gompers, 197
Hobart Gormley "Hobbie", 94-95
Felipe Graciano Jr., 145
David Gurnick, 4
Grant E. Hamilton, 215
Charles K. Harris, 203
Chris Hiatt, 154
Naomi Hirahara, 186
Henry Holt, 142
Langston Hughes, 21
Aldous Huxley, 123
William Lees Judson, 140
Naima J. Keith, 149
William Keith, 152
Helen Keller, 187
Chris Kiefer, 188
Abbot Kinney, 183
Walter Koenig, 159
Tommy Koulax, 160
Josh Kun, 33
Yamila Kun, 54
Norman Lear, 141
Gary Leonard, 161
Liberace, 160
Leo Limón, 126
Belva Ann Lockwood, 174
Matilda Lotz, 175
Charles Lummis, 38
Suzanne Lummis, 207
Guadalupe Mancias, 116
Cheech Marin, 139
Bridget Marrin, 177
Mister Cartoon, 162-163
Richard Montoya, 128
Joseph J. Mora, 192
John Muir, 108
Anna Nelson, 202
Viet Thanh Nguyen, 165
Johnny Oates, 206
Omar Offendum, 115
Esto One, 144
Estevan Oriol, 212
Van Dyke Parks, 112
George C. Perkins, 185
Emilie Stearns Perry, 195
Sebastian S. Petersen, 134
Phantom Street Artist, 121
Susan A. Phillips, 83
Henry Rankin Poore, 147
Adam Princenthal, 191
Tina Princenthal, 191
John Rechy, 208
Frederic Remington, 120
Shizu Saldamando, 113
Abby Sanchez, 18
Peter Shire, 214
Shugga, 122
Stitchin' Sistahz Quilt Circle, 199
John F. Szabo, 15
David L. Ulin, 200
Fernando Valenzuela, 206
Heitor Villa-Lobos, 125
Booker T. Washington, 129
Julia Bracken Wendt, 169
Alden Wood, 31
Kulapat Yantrasast, 118
Robert Ybarra, 50
Yuca's, 48

CREDITS

The autographs featured in *The Autograph Book of L.A.* are from the Autograph Collection, Los Angeles Public Library Special Collections, except as noted below. Most of the photographs included in this book are from The Los Angeles Public Library Photography Collection as detailed below, and other sources for ephemera and some photographs are credited by page.

The author, the Los Angeles Public Library, the Library Foundation of Los Angeles and the publisher are grateful to all who participated in this extensive project.

Autry Museum, Los Angeles: 42 [from Charles F. Lummis Manuscript Collection, Braun Research Library Collection, Autry Museum, Los Angeles; MS.1.10.1, Housebook, p.141]
Josh Kun Collection: 206
Los Angeles Public Library: 29, 223, 224
Los Angeles Public Library Rare Books Department: 22–23, 32, 50, 76, 110–111, 125, 136–137, 178–179, 204–205
Los Angeles Public Library Photography Collection
  Eyre Powell Chamber of Commerce Collection: 34–35
  Herald Examiner Collection: 2, 24–25, 26 (photograph by Chris Gulker), 52 bottom, 56 bottom (photograph by Gene Lester), 66 bottom (photograph by Paul Chinn), 72, 75 top (photograph by Joe Messinger), 75, 80, 81, 98–99
  Los Angeles Neighborhoods Collection: 62 (photograph by Anthony Friedkin)
  Gary Leonard Collection, all photographs by Gary Leonard: 64 bottom, 78, 104–105
  Herman J. Schultheis Collection, photograph by Herman J. Schultheis: 46
  Stone Ishimaru Collection, photograph by Stone Ishimaru: 66 top
  William Reagh Collection, photograph by William Reagh: 64 top
  Security Pacific National Bank Collection: 12–13 (photograph by Stephen Callis), 51, 52 top, 59, 60, 74, 148
  Shades of L.A. Collection: 14–15, 96 (photograph by Ted Merriman), 106–107, 216–217 (photograph Saldana Studio)
  Valley Times Collection: 6–7, 8, 97 (photograph by George Brich)
  Works Progress Administration Collection: 58
Susan A. Phillips (all photographs by Susan A. Phillips): 82–83, 86–87, 88, 90–91, 94–95

The Autograph Book of L.A.: Improvements on the Page of the City
By Josh Kun • Foreword by John F. Szabo • Introduction by Shepard Fairey
Design by Amy Inouye, Future Studio

ISBN 978-1-62640-059-7

Library of Congress Cataloging-in-Publication Data is available.

ACP ANGEL CITY PRESS

Published by Angel City Press
www.angelcitypress.com

Printed in Canada

LOS ANGELES PUBLIC LIBRARY

Library Foundation of Los Angeles

Los Angeles Public Library
Autographs

Improve this page

Los Angeles Public Library
Autographs

Improve this page